The
Martyrs'
Torch

Bruce Porter

Fresh Bread

An Imprint of

Destiny Image® Publishers, Inc.
P.O. Box 310
Shippensburg, PA 17257-0310

ISBN 0-7684-2046-6

For Worldwide Distribution
Printed in the U.S.A.

This book and all other Destiny Image, Revival Press, Fresh Bread, Mercy Place, and Treasure House books are available at Christian bookstores and distributors worldwide.

For a U.S. bookstore nearest you, call **1-800-722-6774**.
For more information on foreign distributors, call **717-532-3040**.
Or reach us on the Internet: **http://www.reapernet.com**

Contact Information for:

Bruce R. Porter

Author of:

The Martyr's Torch

(Destiny Image)

Torchgrab Youth Ministries, Inc.
P.O. Box 621372
Littleton, CO 80162

SPEAKING ENGAGEMENTS
&
"TORCHGRAB"
YOUTH RALLIES

**(Complete Planning Package Featuring Youth
Ministry, Dance/Drama and Music Team)**

ANNOUNCING!

National "Torch Relay Run" to be launched on April 20,
2000 from Littleton, CO to Washington, DC with
Torchgrab Youth Rallies held along the route!

**For Booking Engagements
Contact:
Sherry Snead, Event Coordinator
303-948-7726
Web Site: www.Torchgrab.org**

The Dead

Cassie Bernall
Steven Robert Curnow
Corey DePooter
Kelly Fleming
Matthew Kechter
Daniel Mauser
Daniel Rohrbough
William David Sanders
Rachel Joy Scott
Isaiah Shoels
John Tomlin
Lauren Townsend
Kyle Velasquez

The Wounded

Brian Anderson
Richard Castaldo
Jennifer Doyle
Stephen Austin Eubanks
Nick Foss
Sean Graves
Makai Hall
Anne Marie Hochhalter
Patrick Ireland
Joyce Jankowski
Michael Johnson
Mark Kintgen

Lance Kirklin
Lisa Kreutz
Adam Kyler
Stephanie Munson
Pat Nielson
Nicole Nowlen
Jeanna Park
Kasey Ruegsegger
Valeen Schnurr
Dan Steepleton
Mark Taylor

Publisher's Note

Although the primary figure in *The Martyrs' Torch* is
Rachel Joy Scott, Destiny Image Publishers has endeavored
to honor all thirteen victims of the Columbine tragedy.

Our staff explored many avenues in the attempt to secure
photographs of the other eleven students
and one teacher, but were unsuccessful.
To see pictures and to learn more about each individual,
we refer you to the author's website at
http://www.torchgrab.org

Don Nori
Publisher

iv

Dedication

I dedicate this book to Rachel Joy Scott, whom I have grown to love as my own daughter, and to all the other precious students who were killed or wounded at Columbine. Also, to those teachers who risked their lives to protect their charges, especially to Dave Sanders, who was "killed in action" in a war he didn't choose. Also, to those law enforcement officers, firefighters, and paramedics in our community who placed themselves at risk trying to save our children.

To the parents and family members of those who lost loved ones, my deepest sympathy.

Also, I dedicate this book to Beth Nimmo, Rachel's mom, and to her father, Darrell Scott, who helped bring this "noble soul" into the world. Their commitment to raise Rachel as a godly young woman has enriched us all through the testimony of her life and of her writings.

In addition, this work is dedicated to Pastor Jeff Perry of St. Louis Family Church, who believed in me enough to provide a laptop computer so I could write this book.

v

Finally, I dedicate this book to my loving and patient wife of 23 years, Claudia Jean, whose encouragement and understanding made it possible for me to do this. Without her faithful nudge toward the will of God, this book would never have been written.

All commercial sales royalties from *The Martyr's Torch* will be donated to Rachel Scott's family and carefully chosen charities.

Endorsements

This is no knee-jerk reaction, quickly written book. Bruce Porter, pastor to the family of modern martyr Rachel Joy Scott (slain Columbine High School student) has penned timely but timeless words.

It is *timely* in that it will help us to understand what happened; it's *timeless* in that it puts our present pain in the perspective of the historical Church and its martyrs. We're at the front lines of an intensifying battle where conflicts of values will be ground zero.

As in every battle, there will be victories and there will be casualties. This book helps us to understand the cost of the victory and puts purpose behind the price of the casualty. It should be required reading for the Church. It will cause us to realign ourselves with a reality that much of the Church in the third world nations has already come to terms with: *Martyrdom is as much a part of the future of the Church as it was the history of the Church.*

It's not just a martyr's blood; now it's our martyrs' blood. Perhaps now it can also be our harvest and our revival, reaped from fields fertilized by the blood of modern martyrs like Rachel Scott, Cassie Bernall, and others.

The Body of Christ will be eternally grateful for what the pastor and parents of Rachel Scott share in this book. Insight like this comes from proximity to pain; you pay dearly to pen words like these. None of us would have wanted to pay the high cost of that tuition, but all of us can reap untold benefits from the lessons learned.

"There shall be light at evening time" (see Zech. 14:7b).

We can see the future by the bright light of *The Martyrs' Torch*.

Tommy Tenney
Best-selling author of *The God Chasers*
and *God's Dream Team*

At Rachel Scott's funeral, Bruce Porter delivered a powerful and appropriate message to all of America. The essence of that message is carried out in this book. Bruce challenges us to "take up the torch" the Columbine victims carried and to dedicate our lives to Kingdom purposes.

James Robison
President, LIFE Outreach International
Fort Worth, Texas

This is a book about Columbine, yes, but it is much more. It is a book about the human condition. As Bruce lovingly and honestly writes, events like the Columbine shootings have the power to show us who we really are, but more importantly, they have the power to bring us to God, where we will find answers, hope, and the strength to move on.

Ted Haggard
Senior Pastor, New Life Church
Colorado Springs, Colorado

In the face of the Columbine shooting, churches and faith-based organizations have demonstrated, once again, their vital role in both service and healing. From Rachel Scott's writings we know her to be a young woman on fire for the One she believed in, and it is inspiring to hear of other young people "picking up the torch" that she carried with such passion.

Bill Owens
Governor of Colorado

This is a book for believers and non-believers alike. *The Martyrs' Torch* is a beautiful tribute to the too-short life of an admirable, honest, and heroic young woman, Rachel Joy Scott. We lost her in a tragedy, but it would be a greater tragedy if we did not learn from her example.

Wellington E. Webb
Mayor of Denver

This is indeed a difficult book—hard to read, hard to publish, and obviously, harder to write. The difficulty arises from one source: the incredible, almost incomprehensible barbarism of the tragic Columbine High School massacre of innocents. But you should read it, just as it comes from the heart of a pastor who knew the victims. It may point you toward the imperative change that must be made in American culture today.

D. James Kennedy, Ph.D.
Senior Minister, Coral Ridge Presbyterian Church
Chancellor, Knox Theological Seminary

Stephen was martyred while Paul "looked on." Directly afterward, Stephen's friend, Phillip, rocked the city of Samaria with the gospel. The friends of the Columbine martyrs have begun to shake this nation with the gospel. Bruce Porter tells the story of Columbine in a way that causes many who, like Paul, "look on" as the evil of this generation kills young Christians, to have an encounter with the risen Lord.

Bob Weiner
Rock America Torch Rallies

Pastor Bruce Porter has, with the help of Rachel Scott's writings, captured this unthinkable moment and recorded it here for all eternity. The brutal massacre gives way to hope, salvation, and love through our Savior, Jesus Christ. This tribute will be the definitive work on this pivotal event from which America will rise up and accept *The Martyrs' Torch*.

Gary L. Bauer
Republican Presidential Candidate
Founder, Family Research Council

The tragedy at the Columbine High School brought dark pain. It opened new bleeding wounds in my heart. I, myself, as a pastor, and a parent of children and grandchildren, and a man honored by a Romanian Christian college that bears my name, was deeply touched in reading the book of Pastor Porter. No better words could ever be found than those used by the author—and together with him I try to express the depths of the sorrow and the content of tragedy—in his few lines:

"I sat [in the cemetery]...and wept bitter tears. Tears for Rachel. Tears for Cassie, Kyle, Steven, Lauren, Kelly, and for Mr. Sanders. Tears for Isaiah, Dan, John, Matt, Corey, and Daniel. And yes, even tears for Eric and Dylan, who were lost children growing up in a broken world that sometimes fosters unspeakable evil in those who allow themselves to be enticed by it."

And I add many tears for those not mentioned here. My heart weeps and cries for you, our dear, beloved children. In the darkness and despair, the torch which fell from the dying hands of Rachel brings a ray of light and hope from above:

He healeth the broken in heart, and bindeth up their wounds (Psalm 147:3 KJV).

My help cometh from the Lord, which made heaven and earth (Psalm 121:2 KJV).

The Lord made man out of the dust of the ground as it is told in the Book of Genesis. However, man is not formed simply of the earth (*eretz* in Hebrew, from which the word in English, *earth*, comes). Man formed from the ground is a special Hebrew word, *adamah* (see Gen. 2:9). God used the ground on which the Tree of Life grew and formed man. Man is only a speck of dust in the universe, but what can express his greatness?

Pick up the torch which fell from Rachel's hands, and you will find light and sense for your life. The joys that this world gives are illusory; in the depths of our heart we know that we are sentenced to death and burdened with guilt. When we are light, there is in us the remembrance that we made others weep. Pick up the torch. It brings the light to your consciousness that Jesus our Lord was delivered for our offenses and was raised again for our justification (see Rom. 4:25). Forgiven and renewed, your heart rejoices and begins a new life, being a blessing to all those around you.

The potential of man is huge. There is hope for you. Man must be exceptional, for it is written that the Lord has crowned man with glory and with honor. God has made man a little lower than the angels. Pick up the torch and look to Jesus, your Helper sent from Heaven. The Lord is ready to heal your broken heart. Remember your greatness. There is no time for hatred and quarrel. Remember your greatness, and handle it with cries and prayer. And praise the Creator, who has given to you special gifts to serve Him and your fellowman with "honor and glory."

Pastor Richard Wurmbrand
THE VOICE OF THE MARTYRS

We will not remember 1999 for the parties or the politicians but rather for Pastor Porter's challenge to America's youth to "take up the torch." Some books change your life; other books give you life. *The Martyrs' Torch* is the latter. If your family reads one book (other than the Bible) together in the year 2000, make sure it is *The Martyrs' Torch*. If you are a leader in your community and you fear that a tragedy like the one in Columbine could happen in your school, you must read *The Martyrs' Torch*—a powerful message of hope, purpose, and promise for the new millennium. Pastor Porter challenges all of us—whether we are policymakers or homemakers, fathers, or friends, mothers or ministers, leaders or laypersons—to "take up the torch" and live for God.

No politician, platform, or policy will change your life the way that reading this book will. The tragedy of Columbine continues to ache in the hearts of thousands of Americans. Bruce Porter's words of encouragement and guidance convert tragedy into triumph, helplessness into hope, and pain into purpose. Pastor Porter brings to life the true message of Columbine—that wherever there is affliction and destruction, God's glory, love, and hope stand ready to empower each of us to meet the challenge and "take up the torch."

For America's leaders, the lessons of Columbine are not found in the death and destruction, but in the life and the hope. Pastor Porter's impassioned call for each of us to "take up the torch" is the only law upon which our country can rely to secure our safety and ensure our prosperity. As each shot of the gunmen rang out across our country, our nation's leaders reacted swiftly to the sound of violence with a multitude of policies and promises. However, only Pastor Porter has been able to sift through the wreckage and recover that which the gunmen could not destroy: the spirit, the hope, and the purpose of a few faithful students. Will we, the leaders, "take up their torch"?

Jewell Patek
State Representative
Missouri House of Representatives

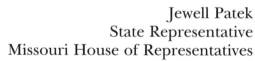

Contents

Foreword

On April 20, 1999, gunshots were fired at Columbine High School in Littleton, Colorado—shots that were heard around the world and that continue to have an immeasurable impact on those left with the horrible consequences of that day. Two high school shooters opened fire on classmates and staff, leaving a trail of 13 dead and many more injured. My 17-year-old daughter, Rachel Joy Scott, was one of those who died that day.

In the days that followed, my family and I began to discover a legacy of journal writings that Rachel left. Although we knew that Rachel was special in so many ways, we were overwhelmed by the evidence of her deep trust and love for Christ. Here was a young girl completely sold out to the Lord, a girl who lived her life with one purpose and goal. That goal was to be used by God to touch her generation with the gospel of Jesus Christ. I have come to the painful realization that Rachel is no longer just a part of our temporal family, but a part of God's eternal plan. It has become increasingly evident that God is honoring Rachel's dreams to reach her generation. My family and I have witnessed the dramatic salvations of literally thousands, the renewal of family values, and a refocusing on Christian principles within our nation, all as a direct result of this tragedy.

The following pages written by our pastor, Bruce Porter, give insight to the days that followed April 20, 1999. He and his beautiful wife, Claudia, walked with our family through our darkest hours. They brought compassionate ministry and comfort in our time of desperate need.

Pastor Bruce has continued to be proactive in showing forth God's purposes of bringing eternal good from this tragedy. This book is just one more testament of those purposes being accomplished.

Beth Nimmo
Mother of Rachel Joy Scott

Lyn Alweis, *The Denver Post*

It is our prayer that memories of the Columbine massacre will not be locked in tragic remorse. This book is offered as a sincere expression of hope and as a challenging question for every reader:

Who will take up the Martyrs' Torch?

The Martyrs' Torch

Precious in the sight of the Lord is the death of His saints (Psalm 116:15 KJV).

And when the Lamb broke the fifth seal, I saw under the altar the souls of all who had been martyred for the word of God and for being faithful in their witness. They called loudly to the Lord and said, "O Sovereign Lord, holy and true, how long will it be before You judge the people who belong to this world for what they have done to us? When will You avenge our blood against these people?" Then a white robe was given to each of them. And they were told to rest a little longer until the full number of the servants of Jesus had been martyred (Revelation 6:9-11).

Rachel Joy Scott began her morning on Tuesday, April 20, 1999, like any other school day. She had breakfast, said good-bye to her mother, Beth, and told her, "I love you" on her way out the door with her 16-year-old brother, Craig. They drove the short distance from their home to Columbine High School together. Rachel parked her car in Clement Park, once again in the same spot as nearly every other day.

John Tomlin, another deeply committed Christian who had recently gone to Mexico on a missions trip and planned to return there one day, parked his truck near Rachel's car. He carefully left a Bible open on his dashboard, obviously in the hope that someone seeing it would think about God that day. Perhaps Rachel and John greeted each other as they grabbed their backpacks and walked together across the park toward the school...and into history. Little did they know that it would be the very last time they would drive to school or stroll together across that grassy knoll. Little did they know that Rachel's car and John's truck, left behind in the parking lot, would soon be photographed icons of human tragedy.

* * * * *

In the early morning hours of January 20, 1999, I awoke from a fitful sleep gasping for air, with deep guttural cries escaping my lips. Bolting upright, heart pounding, I realized that my body was covered in a cold sweat. My dream had frightened me so much that I shook uncontrollably. My wife, hearing my muffled cries, awoke and called out in the darkened bedroom, "Honey, what's wrong?"

I glanced at the clock radio on my bed stand. It was nearly 2:00 a.m. As I tried to calm myself, the images of my dream seemed to superimpose themselves upon the darkened features of my bedroom like ghostly apparitions.

"They were killing, no, slaughtering young people!" I blurted out. "Some of the kids were killing themselves!" I could still see the terrified faces of young men and women, boys and girls actually, bloody and crying. I could yet hear the staccato sounds of gunfire and what seemed to be muffled explosions.

"It was horrible! So real!" I exclaimed. She coached me to remember.

I was in some sort of building. All around me were young people, and although I didn't realize it until later, we were obviously in a school setting. Suddenly several of the youths became bloody, and they began to cry, scream, and run in all directions. I saw what looked like red fire following behind them as they ran, and several fell down. I heard explosions and what sounded like firecrackers.

Suddenly the scene changed, and I saw some young people running in a very peculiar way. They were running in a line, holding their heads...crying, screaming, and praying. Some had blood on their faces, hands, and torsos. I remember thinking, Why would anyone run in such a manner? The horror of that scene was palpable, and I felt their fear and anguish.

Then, as the scene continued to unfold, I saw some of the young people change. They appeared as before, but there seemed to be a look of determined certainty and confidence come over their faces, as if they had remembered something that took away their former terror and replaced it with a steely-eyed focus. I watched several of them turn around and go back into the place they had come from. This time, however, these youths began to give aid to those who had fallen. Some were giving what appeared to be CPR; others were binding wounds while praying and speaking things that seemed to enter into those listening to them like a vapor. There remained conflict, and I could see some of the red flame, but it seemed that a battle had been engaged and that the young people were now winning. I heard a loud voice say, "Rescue 911!"

I had this dream on January 20, 1999, and thankfully, my wife jotted some notes in her journal the next morning and dated it. A few days later I related this dream to a gathering of nearly 15 members of our youth ministry. They seemed interested and somewhat moved, but not particularly alarmed about it. I told them that I rarely have such visions, but that this one *really* got my attention and shook me to the core. I felt that something terrible was about to happen! I simply didn't know where or when.

* * * * *

Three months later to the very day, on Tuesday, April 20, 1999, my entire world changed. I stood sobbing in shocked horror as I watched, with the rest of the world, the television coverage of the Columbine High School massacre.

The young victims who died that day could never have imagined that they would be a part of a worldwide drama that would touch the hearts and lives of millions of people. They were victims of a vicious act of violence, which was perpetrated by other victims who had succumbed to the ageless temptation to lash out and destroy as a result of their inner pain. We have seen the face of unspeakable evil in our community, and we still reel from it.

The believers who allowed their lights to shine so brightly at Columbine High School were soldiers. Oh, they weren't soldiers in the normally accepted sense of the word. Nevertheless, they fought honorably and well on a battlefield that has been created in our nation ever since the 1962 decision by the U.S. Supreme Court to remove prayer from public schools. Their battlefield was their high school, where they engaged an enemy who has cleverly cloaked himself in a disguise of "normal," of "clinical scientific reason," and "secular humanist rationality." They served their King and Lord in a spiritually hostile, toxic environment where the mere mention of the name of Jesus (unless used as a curse word) would instantly elicit derisive ridicule and rejection.

This book is an attempt to share some of my experiences as the pastor of a small local church near Columbine High School. Two of the families attending with us had children at Columbine— the Nimmos and the Suarezes. Javier and Lourdes Suarez had recently emigrated from Mexico with their children, and one of their sons attended Columbine. The Suarez family had the joy of being reunited with their unharmed son.

Larry and Beth Nimmo, the mother and stepfather of Rachel and Craig Scott, had to endure the unspeakable sorrow of losing their 17-year-old daughter Rachel. Also, they have grieved over the horrific trauma inflicted upon their 16-year-old son Craig, who witnessed the death of two of his best friends in the school library.

None of us will ever be the same again. Our lives, along with the lives of each of the victim families, have been altered forever. For most of us, the Lord will bring about a greater expression of His amazing grace. We are finding that God is truly faithful to fulfill His promises.

And we know that God causes everything to work together for the good of those who love God and are called according to His purpose for them (Romans 8:28).

From the moment I heard the news of the shooting, I sensed that this incident of horrific violence was a spiritual event that would potentially change the course of history. It has become something of a spiritual "Pearl Harbor" experience for the Body of Christ in America. As a people, we are being shaken out of our lethargy, complacency, and indifference by this vicious carnage. This is nowhere more evident than in the youth. We are witnessing the birth of a national reformation among young lives.

On the first evening of the Columbine tragedy, I felt strongly compelled to e-mail my closest friends an ongoing series of letters sharing my feelings, observations, sorrows, and impressions as the drama unfolded. Little did I realize in those early morning hours when I finished the first letter and pressed the "send" button on my computer that my little "missive" would be copied, forwarded, and re-sent multiplied thousands of times around the globe! I began to receive phone calls from several continents of the world, and e-mails began pouring in by the hundreds per day! Because of the incredible power of the Internet, multiplied hundreds of thousands of people were reading my letters and weeping with us.

Within the chapters of this book I will share a number of those e-mail updates sent out during the first two months since the Columbine massacre. I've taken the liberty of editing some of the original versions, removing superfluous comments to the e-mail audience, clarifying certain factual inaccuracies, and yet retaining the original spirit and content of the letters. If you have a copy of one of the originals, you are forewarned.

I am often asked how well I knew Rachel. Although her mother and stepfather, Beth and Larry Nimmo, are members of our congregation, I never had the privilege of knowing Rachel in life closely and personally. Rachel was part of a youth group at another church where she and her family had previously attended.

The amazing words Rachel left behind in her journals, together with the vivid and beautiful descriptions of her personality by her family and friends, give me a sense that, somehow, I've known her all her life. My own precious daughter, Naomi, is nearly Rachel's age. I sit and stare at Rachel's picture sometimes and almost get the feeling that she was a daughter I never had the chance to know. I suspect that many parents look at the pictures of these precious young people and feel somewhat the same. After Columbine, Rachel and the others became, in a sense, everyone's kids.

This was a very difficult book to write. I found myself weeping uncontrollably at times as I forced my thoughts into actual printed words. The pain, sorrow, and emotional trauma of this long journey washed over me again as I described what happened. Perhaps this is how I will find my own way to healing. The counselors tell us that we need to find a trusted friend with whom we can share our feelings. I'd like to think that, with this book, I'm sharing with friends who will listen, maybe try to understand, and even weep with me as we walk out this journey together and behold the grace of God in new and fresh ways.

Chapter 1

The End of the World as We Knew It

A day of sorrow is longer than a month of joy.
Chinese proverb

Horror grips us as we watch you die.
All we can do is echo your anguished cries.
Stare, as all human feelings die...
"Wooden Ships"
Crosby, Stills, Nash, and Young
Atlantic Records

It began as a quiet morning, warmed by the beautiful Colorado sunshine illuminating the spring scenery outside my mountain home. I had just refilled my coffee mug after laboring at my home office during the previous hours when the phone rang.

The voice on the other end was frenzied. It was Annette Tiegreen, a dear sister in my church.

"They're killing the kids!" she sobbed. "Turn on the TV!"

She was nearly hysterical, and I just stood there in shocked silence for a moment trying to take in what I had just heard. She screamed into the phone again, "There's gunfire at Columbine High School!"

Dropping the phone, I ran to the television and turned it on. My gaze fell upon scenes that resembled a war movie. SWAT team members were rushing about in black fatigues and Kevlar® helmets, waving automatic weapons. Dozens of ambulances and many, many police and emergency personnel were milling around while helicopters hovered overhead.

> That day will be etched into our collective memory as one of the darkest days in our nation's history.

As my mind tried to take in what my eyes were beholding, the voice-over of the newscaster was describing a vicious attack in progress on the school. Unknown assailants bombed and shot their way through the hallways and classrooms, maiming and killing without mercy nearly everyone they encountered.

That day, April 20, 1999, will be etched into our collective memory as one of the darkest days in our nation's history. I think of it as a spiritual "Pearl Harbor" event, a "mega" wake-up call to us all. As the drama played out in front of the entire world, I stood in the middle of my living room sobbing out prayers for the students, teachers, and rescue workers. What a helpless feeling! Children were being killed, and all we could do was stand by and watch it happen!

"No, Lord!" I cried out over and over again, as if by saying it enough times I could blot out the horrible drama unfolding before me. "How could this be happening in our community?" I sobbed. Our little church was situated a mere half-mile down the street from this school. My thoughts turned to my precious congregation—and to who might have children in that building. From name to name, family to family, face to face, my mind raced.

A short time later my wife, Claudia, came home from her part-time job as a teacher at a local Christian school. Together we began to do roll calls on our membership, desperately trying to think of who might be in danger.

The telephone rang again. The caller informed us that one of our families couldn't find their 17-year-old daughter Rachel. Our hearts sank. Rachel attended Columbine with her 16-year-old brother Craig. As we rushed out to our car, I had an awful sense of foreboding, which I tried to mask from Claudia, not wanting to upset her unnecessarily.

We drove as quickly as we could to the parents' staging center, which was situated at nearby Leawood Elementary School. Those children who had made it out were being bussed to this location and reunited with their frantic parents.

After working our way through the many roadblocks surrounding the area around Columbine, we finally pulled up to Leawood and parked. As I got out of the car, I observed several large satellite uplink vehicles parked around the school with the logos of every major media outlet prominently displayed. Reporters were everywhere doing interviews with various officials and students. We walked quickly past the melee outside and into the building filled with police, counselors, family members, clergy, and school officials.

Quickly moving through the groups of family members in the hallway, Claudia and I walked into the gymnasium. Across the room, I spotted Rachel's mother and stepfather, Beth and Larry Nimmo, standing in the distance. I also saw Rachel's father, Darrell Scott, and several of Rachel's siblings, standing around talking

3

with one another, obviously trying to maintain composure and cling to hope.

As I made my way toward them, one of the victim assist personnel grabbed my arm and took me aside. "Pastor, you need to know before you talk to them that some of the students who escaped said that Rachel was shot. They saw her fall," she said in a hushed voice. "We do not believe she survived."

The room began to swim around me as my heart sank and my eyes welled with tears. I looked over to where the family members stood, so frightened, their eyes searching the crowd for a glimpse of their beloved little girl. I choked back a sob. *How can this be happening, Lord?* I prayed inwardly. *Please help us...help us...* I walked slowly over to Larry and Beth and gathered them in my arms. Beth was crying softly, worry etched upon her face. We prayed together, seeking our Father's mercy and grace to help.

The last busload of children who had escaped the massacre came and left. Rachel's family had stood by and witnessed the joyful reunion of many parents and their terrified children as they bounded off the bus into their eager arms.

Rachel was not among any of them.

After the crowd thinned, Rachel's family sadly stood alone with several other families whose children also had not come, could not come, would never come home again...ever.

Several more hours passed, and the authorities finally convinced everyone that there was nothing more that could be done for the moment. We went to Larry and Beth's home to await word.

As we waited in their home late into the night, I noticed Rachel's younger brother, Craig, pacing the floor, not saying much, and looking devastated. Upon learning that he was also in the school when the massacre occurred, Claudia and I went over to him. I sat down next to Craig where he had plopped down on the piano bench, slipped my arm around his young shoulder, and softly asked him what happened. Nothing in my experience, either as a minister of the gospel or as a Vietnam veteran, could have prepared me for the shocking story Craig began to share between gut-wrenching sobs.

Craig had been sitting in the library with his two friends Matt Kechter and Isaiah Shoels. When the first explosions were heard, they thought it was a senior prank and joked among themselves about it. Suddenly, someone burst into the room, yelling that there were gunmen out in the hallway shooting kids and throwing bombs. The students then collapsed on the floor. Craig, Matt, and Isaiah dove under their tables and tried to hide. Craig said that he heard someone yell that the gunmen were shooting "jocks with white hats." Craig was wearing a white baseball hat that day, and he snatched it off, stuffing it into his shirt just as the gunmen burst into the room.

Eric Harris and Dylan Klebold walked into the library shooting at those they could see and tossing pipe bombs. They were gleefully laughing. "Who's next?" they asked. "Who's ready to die?" They yelled, "All the jocks stand up. We're going to kill every one of you!" They strutted around the room asking people why they should be allowed to live. Some were pleading for their lives, and the killers would say things like, "That's too bad!" Then shots would ring out and there would be silence. They shot again at anyone who groaned or cried. At one point they said, "We've waited to do this a long time." Someone recognized Klebold and asked him, "Dylan, what are you doing!?" Klebold just laughed and said, "Oh, just killing some people." Witnesses observed that there was not a hint of conscience, mercy, or remorse as Eric and Dylan shot person after person in their rampage.

Craig and his friends were still hiding under the table. As Eric and Dylan approached, Craig heard one of them say, "Hey, there's a n—— under here!" Isaiah Shoels, a black student, said nothing as the merciless blast of the shotgun tore into his body. As he fell next to Craig dying, Craig fell too and played dead. The killers then leveled their weapons on Matt Kechter, slaying him. Craig sobbed convulsively as he told of hearing his two friends gasping for air as life departed from their shattered bodies.

Laughing at the dying victims and making mocking comments about their torn bodies, Harris and Klebold moved on to other students in the room who were frantically trying to find cover.

Kasey Ruegsegger, a beautiful girl with strong faith, was hiding under a table. When she first heard the gunfire and Harris and Klebold burst into the room, she said that she knew she was going to be shot. However, she also felt the presence of God with her, and later she said she knew He would be with her through it all. She was shot in her shoulder, hands, and neck. Kasey began to moan from the pain. "Shut up and quit bitching!" one of the killers shouted. She fell backward and pretended to be dead. Harris and Klebold moved on. Miraculously, she survived.

At one point they encountered Cassie Bernall, who was reading her Bible when the shooting began. What happened next is somewhat unclear. The girl under the table with Cassie said that Cassie was praying fervently as the killers stormed around the room, shooting classmates. This girl stated that Cassie said nothing at all when one of the killers looked under the table where they were hiding, said "peekaboo," and shot Cassie, killing her instantly. Other students claim that one of the killers confronted Cassie with a taunting question: "Do you believe in God?" Cassie has been popularly attributed with saying the words: "Yes, I do believe in God!" The killer then reportedly sneered, "Why?"

One student, from his position across the room, heard these words exchanged and thought it was Cassie who said them. However, when the police asked him to point out the position in the library where he believed the words had come from, he indicated the position where another girl, Valeen Schnurr, had been hiding. As you will read, Valeen, who survived her massive wounds, had a verbal exchange with one of the killers in which the exact words attributed to Cassie were spoken.

It matters little in the end whether or not Cassie was quoted correctly in this circumstance. The fact that so many who knew her instantly accepted the initial reports that she said "yes" is a clear indication that, without any doubt whatsoever, she would have said it! Cassie's mother, Misty Bernall, in her highly recommended book, *She Said Yes*, made it clear that Cassie said, "yes" every day. In any case, several student eyewitnesses in the library maintain that they heard both Cassie and Valeen questioned about their faith in God. Both said, "yes."

Valeen was studying in the library with her best friend, Lauren Townsend, that morning. When someone ran in yelling about a gunman and warning the students to take cover, Valeen and Lauren hid under a table together, listening to the bombs exploding downstairs.

She watched from her hiding place as Harris and Klebold came into the library and walked past the area where she and Lauren hid. She thinks they threw a pipe bomb because she saw books flying across the room.

What happened next was an absolute nightmare. She could hear other students being shot as they pleaded for their lives. Harris and Klebold would mock them before shooting and say, "You don't want to die? Well, that's just too bad!" Some screams coming from her end of the room drew the gunmen's attention, and they began to spray their hiding place with bullets and throwing pipe bombs, which peppered everything with shrapnel.

Multiple bullets and shrapnel hit Valeen, and she slumped and clutched her abdomen. The doctors later reported that she was hit more than 15 times by bullets and fragments. "Oh my God, oh my God!" she cried out from the pain.

7

Her cries caught the attention of the killers. "God?" one of the gunmen taunted her. "Do you really believe in God?"

She later told her mother that she was afraid to say "yes," but that she was also afraid to say "no," because she thought she was dying.

Finally, looking up at the gunman, she told him, "Yes, I believe in God."

"Why?" he asked, pausing to reload his weapon.

"My parents brought me up that way," she said. "And I believe." She remembers babbling on for a few seconds after that, and then crawling away under a table.

Inexplicably, the gunman turned and walked away. Valeen lay under the table, holding her friend Lauren's hand. She then heard someone yelling that the killers had left the room. She reached out a bloodstained hand and tenderly touched Lauren's face. "Wake up, Lauren, it's time to get out!" she said. Lauren didn't move. Valeen tried to wake her up, but Lauren would never wake up in this world again. Lauren was gone.

Valeen wrapped her sweatshirt around her abdomen, trying to stop the profuse bleeding from multiple bullet and shrapnel wounds. With all her remaining strength, she tried to carry her friend Lauren out to safety. After struggling frantically with Lauren's body, Valeen realized that she was simply too weak and had to leave her best friend behind.

Valeen spoke of her experience publicly for the first time at our Columbine Torchgrab Youth Rally in Littleton on August 7. The following is a partial transcript of her remarks that morning.

"...Only when I look back at the events that took place that day do I see Columbine at the mercy of a spiritual war. So many battles took place that day: the battle between good and evil, my personal battle to

8

fight to stay alive after being shot numerous times, and also, the fight to stand for what I believe, even if it meant to die for it.

"When I laid there, and those two boys asked me if I believed in God, I wanted so much to say 'no.' So much—I had so much fear inside that I didn't know what to do. I looked toward them and said the only thing I could say—because to say 'no' would be disrespectful for myself and to my God. I looked toward them and I said, 'yes,' and then they asked me 'why?' I said, 'My parents brought me up that way and—because I believe.'

"To this day I always wonder why they left me alone. I should be dead. But I know that God has me here for a reason today—

"Even though this chapter of this war has been fought, there is yet another fight to be won, and every one of you guys are going to be fighting this fight when you go back to school this month.

"The problems that led to the tragedy at Columbine are the same problems we see in every school across the nation. The lack of tolerance and acceptance, and the disrespect we have for one another— these are the intangible problems that the government cannot solve through gun control and legislation or safety issues in our schools. They are the problems that have to be solved through ourselves, and in our hearts. The ones with faith [are those] who can make a difference in today's society."

* * * * *

As the killers moved on out of the library searching for more victims, Craig Scott, his ears still ringing from the blasts of the shotgun that killed his friends, said how he heard the voice of God say to him, "Get up and get out now!" As he scrambled to his feet, he saw several horribly wounded students around him, including 17-year-old Kasey Ruegsegger, whose arm was nearly blown off at the shoulder from a shotgun blast. Craig recounted, "She had a chunk of her shoulder blown off with a shotgun, and I helped her get out. She was bleeding all over the place and her shoulder bone was showing." She was weakly calling out, "Help me, help me." Craig grabbed her, carefully cradling her arm, and began to help her and other students out to safety.

My wife and I were the very first persons in the world to hear Craig's terrifying story that evening as he sobbed and cried. "I couldn't find Rachel! I prayed with a bunch of other kids that they'd find their brothers and sisters, and I even helped them out of the building. I said, 'See, God really answers our prayers!' but I just couldn't find Rachel anywhere!" I put my arm around this young man's shoulder and wept with him. Youthful naiveté vanished forever that day.

Claudia and I rode silently to our home very late that night with heavy, broken hearts. How could we find sleep after all that had happened? When I walked into my house, I felt a compelling, urgent pull toward my computer. It seemed as if the Holy Spirit was moving upon me to sit down and write what I had just experienced. Although I was bone tired, I turned it on. As the screen came to life, I sensed that the Lord wanted me to write an e-mail to my close friends on our e-mail list. I wrote the following:

E-mail Update
Wednesday morning, April 21, 1999, 2:30 a.m.

My heart is broken, but Christ remains my strength...

I just returned from a heart-wrenching time sitting with, and ministering to, the families of those whose children were not yet accounted for. One of these was a precious family from my church. Two of their children attended Columbine High School where a most horrible slaughter of innocents took place today.

One of them, Craig Scott, a wonderful young man of 16 tender years, told my wife, Claudia, and I through gut-wrenching sobs of watching his friends brutally murdered right in front of his eyes. He had to lie still in the blood of his dying friends, feigning death, so that the demons who laughed as they shot and killed kids all around them would pass him by. After the murderers left the room in search of more victims, this young man got to his feet and tried to help his fellow students escape. He helped one young girl, whose arm was nearly blown off by a shotgun blast, to safety. He prayed for the Lord's strength as he found survivors and pushed them outside. He was a hero today. He came home.

Rachel, his beautiful 17-year-old sister, didn't come home tonight.

Several students who survived said they saw her fall, mortally wounded. She loves Jesus fervently, and tonight she may be dancing and rejoicing in His glorious presence. My heart is breaking for her mom and dad and her brothers and her family. We sat in a staging area at Leawood Elementary School for hours awaiting word of her. None came. Tonight, Claudia and I went to Rachel's home and prayed, and cried, and watched the news with her family. We will know for sure later this morning where Rachel is. In my spirit, I already know.

Please pray for the broken people of our community. I'm exhausted. Tomorrow will bring fresh grace and mercy. We'll all need it for sure...

Pastor Bruce

"And God will wipe away every tear from their eyes; there shall be no more death, nor sorrow, nor crying. There shall be no more pain, for the former things have passed away." Then He who sat on the throne said, *"Behold, I make all things new."* And He said to me, *"Write, for these words are true and faithful"* (Revelation 21:4-5 NKJV).

"I am now going to see that head that was crowned with thorns, and see the face that was spit upon for me. I have formerly lived by hearsay and faith, but now I go where I shall live by sight, and shall be with Him in whose company I delight myself." (Mr. Standfast, one of the great characters in *Pilgrim's Progress* by John Bunyan)

11

Chapter 2

A Heartbroken Community

God's Loan

"I'll lend to you for a little time,
A child of mine," He said,
"For you to love the while she lives
And mourn for when she's dead.
It may be six or seven years
Or twenty-two or three,
But will you till I call her back,
Take care of her for me?
She'll bring her charms to gladden you
And should her stay be brief,
You'll have these precious memories,
As solace for your grief.

I cannot promise she will stay
Since all from earth return.
But there are lessons taught down there
I want this child to learn.
I've looked this whole world over,
In my search for teachers true.
And in the crowds that throng life's land,
I have selected you.
Now will you give her all your love
Not think the labor vain,
Nor hate me when I come to call
To take her back again?"
It seems to me I heard them say,
"Dear Lord, Thy will be done.
For all the joys thy child shall bring,
The risk of grief we'll run.
We'll shelter her with tenderness,
We'll love her while we may,
And for the happiness we've known
Forever grateful stay.
And should the angels call for her
Much sooner than we've planned,
We'll brave the bitter grief that comes
And try to understand."
Author Unknown
(Parson's Bible Illustrator, index #2162)

The Lord gets His best soldiers out of the highlights of affliction.
Charles H. Spurgeon

Claudia and I slept fitfully for only a few hours before rising again to go back to Beth and Larry's to await word of Rachel. On our way to their home, we stopped at the local Albertson's grocery store to pick up some food for their family. To our amazement, when the store manager learned that we were purchasing some food for one of the victim families, he refused payment and filled our shopping cart. Such acts of kindness were repeated across our community in the coming weeks.

As we pulled up in front of Rachel's family home that morning, there were cars up and down the street. Relatives from everywhere were arriving to hold vigil with the family. We took the food inside and spent the next several hours talking and praying with family members, listening to their stories, and hoping against hope that somehow Rachel would be found alive.

It wasn't until midday that official word finally came. Our worst fears were confirmed. Rachel was gone. God's holy angels had carried her away from her bullet-riddled, lifeless earthly tent. Flying far above the chaos, far above the mayhem and madness of this present twisted and unworthy world, Rachel had been delivered tenderly into the arms of Him whom she once worshiped by faith, to behold Him face-to-face in all His majesty and glory: Jesus, whom she loved more than life itself.

The tears flowed freely from a heartbroken grief that only a loving parent who has lost a child could ever begin to understand. As a minister I have learned that, at such times, no words can suffice to comfort; no expressions of condolence can assuage the pain. Such tears are holy things in the sight of God, and all one can hope to do in such moments is to "weep with those who weep."[1]

On that bitter day, April 21, 1999, a collective wail of mourning was heard throughout our community. Families of Littleton raised their voices in an ancient chorus of sorrow and partook together the bitter cup of mourning, accompanied by an entire nation.

The days following were filled with the grace of God as multitudes of His people from around the world lifted a concert of intercession and supplication unto the very heights of Heaven itself. Along with the other families in Littleton who had lost their precious children, Rachel's family walked the bitter path of funeral preparations with grace beyond human strength. All of us commented about the strength that seemed to flow toward us, and there was a growing sense of God's presence and purpose in all that ensued.

Before the memorial service on Wednesday evening, I had a growing sense that God was at work behind the scenes and was going to bring forth a much larger purpose through all that had happened. When I rose to speak, I surveyed the sea of youthful faces before me, and I felt a stirring within. *Could this be the generation, Lord?* I wondered. *Could this be the mighty army You promised that would come forth in the last days to carry Your banner?* I hadn't quite put to words what I was sensing, but I felt that there was a cause, a vision, and a banner that this generation was to take up. I struggled inwardly to discover the word-picture that God seemed to be imparting to my heart.

My message to the youth that night was rather aggressive for a memorial setting, even in my own hearing. I felt some sort of message trying to be birthed in my heart, but my mind couldn't completely get around it. I urged the students to turn the situation around and make the dark forces of evil pay for what they did. I felt a rally cry coming forth, and many told me later that the spirit in which I shared really stirred up feelings of wanting to do something about what had happened to the victims.

E-mail Update
Thursday morning, April 22, 1999, 1:30 a.m.

I'm very tired, having just returned from a memorial service this past evening. It's been a very long day, but I wanted to give you an update before retiring.

As of this morning Rachel Scott's family still hadn't received official word of their daughter's death. The waiting was agonizing, but after 1:00 p.m. this afternoon, I received a call from the Coroner's office confirming officially that Rachel's body had been positively identified.

16

Although she was already fairly convinced that Rachel was with the Lord, it was very difficult delivering that news of finality to Rachel's mom. We spent several hours praying and weeping with the family members who had assembled in their home. Pictures of Rachel adorned the living room. She was such a beautiful 17-year-old! We spent time praying together and seeking our Father's merciful comfort.

This evening we joined another church in holding a memorial service for Rachel and the other students killed or wounded. Over 1,500 people attended. We heard stories of several students who survived while their classmates were slaughtered as they begged for their lives. I had the honor of addressing this assembly for 20 minutes, and I urged that we all receive the grace of Jesus to heal our wounds and resurrect our community out of this morass of pain and confusion. One of the ways we must find healing is in forgiving those who have hurt us. There seemed to be a special presence of the Lord this evening upon us all.

This Saturday we will hold a funeral service for Rachel at 1:30 p.m. We expect the Lord to bring many young people to Himself through this service. Never before have we seen such an open hunger for God in the young people of this community!

Thank you for all your prayers and thoughtful notes. Please continue. The process of healing the scars of this tragedy will take time and lots of prayer.

Pastor Bruce Porter

One of the most agonizing things that the victim parents had to endure was the long wait to obtain news of their children. Just the thought that their children were so grievously wounded, and quite likely dead, lying in a pool of blood somewhere, and to be helpless to go to them, is beyond human comprehension. Because of the nature of the crime and the fact that the carnage was so extensive, the authorities had sealed the school and immediate surroundings. The pain for Rachel's family was beyond words. The wait was agonizing.

As it happened, we had already seen Rachel's lifeless body that first evening being dragged by two SWAT team members on television. We all thought it was the body of a young man, as the team had the body by the arms, face down, trying, I suppose, to gain a safer vantage point so they could determine her condition. When Rachel's family saw the live images, one of her sisters commented that it looked like Rachel.

Everyone was in shock. No one wanted to believe that the small, frail, and obviously lifeless body being shown on national TV was indeed Rachel. It was confirmed later, and one of the officers who so heroically risked his own safety in an ill-fated effort to save her life was later plagued with guilt and remorse. Most people have no comprehension of how difficult it is for law enforcement and emergency services personnel to cope with such carnage.

Some time later, with her parents' permission, I had opportunity to read the autopsy report from the Coroner's office. We wanted to gain some understanding of the exact circumstances of her death, in order to try to clarify several rumors regarding possible verbal exchanges she may have had with her killers. It was extremely painful to read the details of her wounds and to know how this young woman died. She had been shot four times with a 9mm weapon. It appears that the final shot was to her head. This gives some credence to the initial report that Rachel had exchanged words with her assailant before she expired. Her mother was at least comforted that she hadn't suffered long. However, as I will demonstrate later, Rachel appeared to have already settled the issue of her death long before it occurred.

"Lord, remind me how brief my time on earth will be. Remind me that my days are numbered, and that my life is fleeing away. My life is no longer than the width of my hand. An entire lifetime is just a moment to You; human existence is but a breath."

18

We are merely moving shadows, and all our busy rushing ends in nothing. We heap up wealth for someone else to spend. And so, Lord, where do I put my hope? My only hope is in You (Psalm 39:4-7).

E-mail Update
Friday morning, April 23, 1999, 1:00 a.m.

So many have contacted us in the last 24 hours from around the world expressing grief, sorrow, and condolences. We quite simply cannot respond to each one personally. I will try to bring you up-to-date on the recent developments of the day. The family of 17-year-old Rachel Scott, who died in the massacre, expresses their sincere thanks to all who have prayed for them during this incredibly difficult time.

Today Rachel's family had to move through the painful process of planning the funeral. With meetings all day long with funeral personnel and those of us who will officiate the funeral service, Rachel's parents were quite exhausted. The highlight of the day was an amazingly anointed interview with CBN News. The CBN staff was so sensitive to the family, and I could see that the Lord was beginning to work a healing in Rachel's parents as they shared their pain.

Rachel's body was released by the Coroner's office this afternoon to the funeral home. The family had the opportunity to view her body Friday afternoon. This was an important part of closure for them.

The funeral for Rachel Scott will be held this Saturday. From 9:30 a.m. to 12:30 p.m. Rachel's casket will be placed in the church sanctuary and made available to the public for viewing. Friends, schoolmates, teachers, and relatives are invited to write their thoughts and good-byes on the casket. The funeral service will begin at 1:30 p.m.

Please pray for all of us who will be sharing, that the Lord will strengthen and inspire us to speak words of comfort, healing, and faithful testimony of Jesus.

"And pray for us, too, that God may open a door for our message, so that we may proclaim the mystery of Christ, for which I am in chains. Pray that I may proclaim it clearly, as I should" (Colossians 4:3-4 NIV).

"For there is a wide-open door for a great work here, and many people are responding. But there are many who oppose me" (1 Corinthians 16:9).

Thanks for your continued prayers,
Pastor Bruce Porter

Endnotes

1. Romans 12:15 NKJV.

Chapter 3

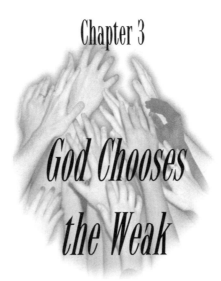

God Chooses the Weak

For a great and effective door has opened to me,
and there are many adversaries.
(1 Corinthians 16:9 NKJV)

Rachel's mother, Beth, had asked me to preside over Rachel's funeral, along with two other local pastors and friends, Billy Epperhart of Trinity Christian Center and Barry Palser of Orchard Road Christian Center. Both of these churches had played a large part in the spiritual life of Rachel's family over the years, and it was more than fitting that we minister together to the family during this time. Rachel attended Barry's youth group at Orchard Road, and several of the other family members attended Billy's church. Billy's church was the largest facility available in the area, and he was more than gracious in making his building and staff available to Rachel's family and friends.

As I prayed on Friday evening, seeking to prepare myself for the funeral, my spirit and mind were deeply troubled. The events of the previous days and the sheer magnitude of the tragedy seemed to bear down so heavily upon my heart that I desperately cried out to the Lord for His strength. I sensed the presence of God there in my study in a very unique and powerful way, and I fell to the floor, sobbing in deep intercession. I don't usually have such experiences, but on this particular night I sensed that the Holy Spirit was imparting an unusual anointing upon me.

The stirring in my heart that I had felt before the Wednesday night memorial service was growing in its intensity. A rally cry was rising within my spirit. My mind became filled with a vision of a torch, blazing in brilliant light. As I pondered this, my thoughts turned toward the idea that each believer is a bearer of the light of the good news of Christ's redemption for all mankind. We are each stewards of the light of the gospel, which has been passed down for nearly 2,000 years to each successive generation of believers. As Jesus said,

> *You are the light of the world–like a city on a mountain, glowing in the night for all to see. Don't hide your light under a basket! Instead, put it on a stand and let it shine for all* (Matthew 5:14-15).

I thought of Columbine's slain and how many of them had been such a light to their fellow students for the gospel. In truth, they had carried that ancient bloodstained torch through the halls of Columbine. The Lord impressed upon me that the torch of the gospel of the grace of God had fallen from the hands of these young witnesses! As soon as I saw this, I knew what my message was to be at Rachel's funeral.

During the entire night, I seemed to hear the Lord's gentle voice speaking to my heart and leading me as to what I should say.

I was clearly instructed not to make too many notes, beyond a few quotes that I felt impressed to share. In the Book of Jeremiah we read of the promise God made to this young man that he was to lean heavily upon God to give him the words he should speak.

> *But the Lord said to me: "Do not say, 'I am a youth,' for you shall go to all to whom I send you, and whatever I command you, you shall speak. Do not be afraid of their faces, for I am with you to deliver you," says the Lord. Then the Lord put forth His hand and touched my mouth, and the Lord said to me: "Behold, I have put My words in your mouth"* (Jeremiah 1:7-9 NKJV).

*   *   *   *   *

I believe that there is a facet of humility that is vitally important for anyone who desires to be a speaker of the cause of Christ. That facet is the realization that God can and will speak through a yielded person who has a healthy distrust in his own ability or resourcefulness. We ministers, especially those of us who have been around for a number of years, easily fall into familiar patterns of ministry that can actually mimic the power and anointing of God. This is dangerous, for it is possible to get up and say things in the name of the Lord that the Lord isn't saying!

> *Are you called to be a speaker? Then speak as though God Himself were speaking through you. Are you called to help others? Do it with all the strength and energy that God supplies. Then God will be given glory in everything through Jesus Christ. All glory and power belong to Him forever and ever. Amen* (1 Peter 4:11).

The little donkey who carried Jesus into Jerusalem would have been very foolish if he'd entertained the thought that all those cheering people along the pathway were excited about him!

This is humility, and my heart yearns for it! In those moments when I am enabled by the grace of God to completely acknowledge my personal weakness, it's then that my Father seems to rush in by His mighty Spirit and fill me afresh with true power and authority. We don't really come to the beginning of God until we come to the end of ourselves. That kind of authority doesn't need much help from public relations firms or slick promotions. Most people are sharp enough to know when they're smelling the aroma of "fresh bread," and they will automatically shun the moldy, stale, religious stuff they've been force-fed for so many years.

*   *   *   *   *

Well, in spite of the fact that I had slept no more than two hours during the night, I arose refreshed Saturday morning. I sensed a deep and abiding anointing and presence of the Lord upon me. I felt a supernatural confidence and boldness. It no longer seemed to matter that I would be speaking that day to such a huge multitude. My heart was at peace. I went to my computer and wrote...

E-mail Update
Saturday morning, April 24, 1999, 7:00 a.m.

We are so thankful for the multitudes of expressions of love and prayer and support during these past few days. I have tried to express the sheer magnitude of the responses to the Scott family, and they expressed their thanks for your care and concern. They cannot read the individual notes right at the moment, but are comforted by them and will draw strength from them in the weeks and months to come.

I wanted to give a quick update on things here and request your prayers for us as we prepare to minister at Rachel's funeral this afternoon. So much has been happening in the past 24 hours, and we are definitely feeling buoyed by the prayers of the saints. I sometimes have the strange feeling of being a separated spectator watching myself saying and doing things. Very weird. God's grace is abundant.

Yesterday was really hard for Rachel's family. We met with them for a few hours, talking of Rachel's life, reminiscing, laughing, crying, and remembering this very unique person. I was awestruck listening to her sisters and brothers tell of what a wonderful and sweet sister she was. Mom and Dad related many happy memories and some really funny stories of her growing up. How could such a sweet, beautiful young woman die like this?

Afterward, the time came to go to the funeral home and view Rachel's earthly tent for the first time since her death. The last her mom had seen her was Tuesday morning as she went off to school. As the family gathered around her body, you could almost hear the flutter of angelic wings enfolding them all in a soft glow of heavenly light. The presence of God was tangible, and I had to lower my eyes in that holy effulgence. Holy are the tears of God's saints. Precious in the eyes of the Lord is the blood of His martyrs.

Today is the funeral. We are walking this out by faith. It begins at 1:30 p.m. local time. CNN will be broadcasting from the funeral as a part of a press pool, and there is every possibility that millions will be joining with us as we mourn Rachel and the other students who were slain. Pray that we will be able to speak into the hearts of multiplied millions of young people the reality of Christ's love for them and the need for them to turn their backs on hate, death, and violence.

The crushing weight of a sense of responsibility would be overwhelming if it were not for the prayers of so many. We're praying that our poor words will somehow be used by God to spark a spiritual revolution in the youth of America. They, and only they, can change things in their generation with the help of God. I'm praying for a multitude of young people to be touched by Rachel's example and take up the bloodstained torch that fell from her hand and make it burn brightly for Christ!

Please feel free to forward this message to any you feel led to. This could be an hour of great victory for Christ in our nation. With your prayers, and the grace of God, it will be...

Sincerely in Jesus' love and blessing,
Pastor Bruce Porter

Chapter 4

An Autographed Casket

...Yet who knows whether you have come
to the kingdom for such a time as this?
(Esther 4:14 NKJV)

When Claudia and I arrived at the funeral, many, many hundreds of people were already there. Rachel's coffin was sitting closed at the front of the room, lovingly framed with some of the most beautiful flower arrangements I have ever seen. The casket was a very special one, constructed of light materials and textured so that people could write upon it with markers their thoughts and prayers. It was heart wrenching to read some of the inscriptions, written personally to Rachel from her mom and dad, sisters and brothers, aunts and uncles, cousins and friends. There were such beautiful, yet heartbreaking inscriptions, lovingly scribbled by

27

hands made unsteady by crushing grief and sorrow. By the time the funeral began, Rachel's casket was literally covered with such prayers, good-byes, and personal expressions of grief that even the angels must have wept! These words would accompany her body into the earth.

The service itself was overwhelmingly emotional from beginning to end. The music, words of love spoken by family and friends, videos of family photos, and messages from everyone who shared their hearts, touched me deeply. I sat on the platform frequently choking back sobs, trying to remain composed in the face of such overwhelming sorrow and loss. It seemed that the entire world was weeping with us as we made our way through the ceremony. I recall looking out over the congregation and beholding the universal grief etched on every face. Even the little children were unusually quiet and subdued. I glanced down at the seemingly endless rows of moms and dads, grandmas and grandpas, children and high school students. Some sat staring ahead, as if in a daze; others held their faces in their hands, weeping silently. In such times we humans find an unusual sense of unity and oneness, and, in spite of our many differences, we are bound together by our shared pain of living in a sin-sick, broken world. The crowd was so large that an overflow room had been arranged for people to view the service on a giant-screen television monitor.

As the time approached for me to speak, I felt again that wonderful, special, almost giddy sense of the presence of God upon me. I suppose that there are many words in the languages of man that might describe what I felt at that moment, but the most accurate description I can come up with now is simply this...

I felt...loved.

When people imagine what it's like to be in the presence of God, or to sense His anointing, one often hears a wide range of ideas. Some describe God as all-powerful, and He certainly is that. Others describe His majesty and holiness. These are also certainly a part. Even others are fascinated by His awesome wisdom and understanding. Truly His ways are definitely past finding out.

I can't speak for anyone else, but for me, I know I'm in the presence of God when I feel loved. It's a certain sense of supernatural confidence, acceptance, security, peace of mind, and joy. I imagine it's like the feeling a baby has when enfolded close to his mother's breast: warm, secure, close, accepted, provided for, protected, and unafraid. The first time that sense of well-being came over me was when I accepted the grace and forgiveness in Jesus Christ in 1973, and I *knew* I was at peace with God.

The same feeling of God's love flooded my being at Rachel's funeral. Conscious of multitudes of people praying for me at that moment, I rose to speak, my mind strangely at peace. Stepping up to the podium, I opened my Bible, took out my brief notes, and opened my mouth in faith...

Transcript of Funeral Remarks

"At this time in the service, we've made space for any family members of Rachel to have an opportunity to share any comments that they may have at this time. I know it's very difficult for you, but if you do, we want to give you that opportunity. [Short pause; no response from family.] All right.

"This tragedy in our community has shaken all of us to the very core of our being. As I received communications, as we have ministered to the family, from literally from all over the world, people have sent in their cards and their condolences, their e-mails, and we all live in a state of shock at this time. It's a very difficult time for us. We have so many questions that are unanswered, so many things within our hearts that we're looking to God and asking Him: What is Your wisdom?

Craig F. Walker, *The Denver Post*

What is wrong that such brutality can take place among our children?

"I would like to read to you from Psalm 64 [NIV]:

Hear me, O God, as I voice my complaint; protect my life from the threat of the enemy. Hide me from the conspiracy of the wicked, from that noisy crowd of evildoers. They sharpen their tongues like swords and aim their words like deadly arrows. They shoot from ambush at the innocent...they shoot at [them] suddenly, without fear. They encourage each other in evil plans, they talk about hiding their snares; they say, "Who will see them?" They plot injustice and say, "We have devised a perfect plan!" Surely the mind and heart of man are cunning. But God will shoot them with arrows; suddenly they will be struck down. He will turn their own tongues against them and bring them to ruin; all who see them will shake their heads in scorn. All mankind will fear; they will proclaim the works of God and ponder what He has done. Let the righteous rejoice in the Lord and take refuge in Him; let all the upright in heart praise Him!

"We've heard so many honoring words about Rachel. And many of you have seen the interviews with members of her family, and you've been touched.

"I want to say, on behalf of the family, a heartfelt thank you for each and every one of you who have prayed for them and stood with them and the other families of this terrible tragedy that our community has endured.

"We want to honor Rachel, primarily, here. But it's vitally important that we ask ourselves some hard questions: What has happened to us as a people, that this should happen to us? What is wrong that such brutality can take place among our children?

"I look at my own son and daughter present here today— a 16- and an 18-year-old—and when this terrible tragedy happened, I hugged them so long they almost needed CPR when I was finished, because I was so glad to see them. What has happened to us? How did we get here?

"We removed the Ten Commandments from our schools. In exchange, we've reaped selfish indifference and glorified hedonism.

"We've told our children that they were nothing more than highly evolved amoebae, accidentally brought forth from a mud pool somewhere in time. And we wonder why so many of them see no intrinsic value to life.

"We removed prayer from our schools and we've reaped violence, and hatred and murder. And we have the fruit of those activities before us now.

"I want to say to you here today, that prayer was established again in our public schools last Tuesday.

[APPLAUSE]

"What the judiciary couldn't do, what the churches couldn't do, the children did themselves.

[APPLAUSE]

"The Duke of Wellington once said, 'If you divorce religion from education, you produce a race of clever devils.' The young men who perpetrated this terrible crime were highly intelligent people. It may interest you to know, because they perpetrated this on Hitler's birthday, that over 40 percent of the German Gestapo had graduate degrees.

"There are many who say that all we need is better education. 'Let's throw more money at schools; let's have Internet and computers, and then we'll be all right'—but it doesn't touch the heart of our children. There's an issue of character here.

"It's so simplistic for us to say, 'Let's remove the weapons of destruction from their hands' and not deal with the hardness and depth of despair in the hearts. This can only be done as Rachel knew: by trusting in a loving and compassionate God.

"I found an interesting quote from a school principal who survived a Nazi concentration camp, and he once wrote this advice to his teachers:

> 'Dear teachers, I am the survivor of a concentration camp. My eyes saw what no man should witness—gas chambers built by learned engineers, children poisoned by educated physicians, infants killed by trained nurses, women and babies shot and burned by high school and college students. So I am suspicious of education.
>
> 'My request is; help your students become humane. Your efforts must never produce learned monsters, skilled psychopaths, educated Eichmanns. Reading, writing, arithmetic are important only if they serve to make our children more humane.'

"Rachel, as you have heard here today, personified the love and the grace of God, and as we have come to know her, and appreciate the commitment that she made to become a believer in Jesus Christ over four and a half years ago, a conversion that was so powerful that the people who saw her when it happened said this was very unusual. Her commitment has been lived out before all of us, and she's been a light to everyone who knows her.

"She was a warrior, but she didn't fight her war with guns and with instruments of destruction. Rachel fought with the implements of love and compassion and caring mercy. She loved everyone she met. But as a warrior, Rachel carried a torch that was stained by the blood of the martyrs from the very first day of the Church's existence in the world nearly 2,000 years ago. This warrior has now dropped that torch and gone on to her eternal reward.

"Young people here today, hear me. I want to issue a challenge to each and every one of you. Don't despair of life. Don't despair of what's happened to you. Rachel carried a torch—a torch of truth, a torch of compassion, a torch of love, a torch of the good news of Jesus Christ her Lord, whom she was not ashamed of, even in her hour of death. I want to lay a challenge before each and every one of you young people here today: The torch has fallen from Rachel's hand. Who will pick it up again? Who will pick up the torch again?

Courtesy of Beth Nimmo

**Rachel Joy Scott
junior photo**

"Students, as well meaning as our politicians have been, they couldn't protect you. As well meaning as our police— and I'm a volunteer fireman—we couldn't help you. The police did all they possibly could. The legislators had laws in place that should have protected you already, and the laws didn't protect you. And I want to ask your forgiveness on behalf of many of us who are parents. Forgive us because we failed you. We failed Rachel.

"It's up to you. If you're going to take your schools back, you have to do it. If there's a stand to be taken, it can't be taken by politicians, as well meaning as they may be, or by legislators or by the police or by even your parents. Students, you have to take the stand. It's your school!

[Applause]

"I am hereby issuing a challenge to every student in every school across this nation. Pick up the torch that Rachel carried. Pick it up and hold it high and stop being a victim. Be proactive, speak to the culture you live in, declare a 'cultural revolution' of compassion and mercy and love and forsake violence. You have the power within your hands, young people. We can't do it. We have failed.

"I want to know right now who will take up that torch. Let me see you. Stand up. Who will pick up Rachel's torch? Who will do it? Hold it high!

[Young people by the hundreds leap to their feet in the auditorium. Applause]

"Hold up that torch right now! If you are watching from some other place, stand up where you are, stand up and say: 'I won't be a victim! I will lift that torch high! The love of Jesus!'

"I want you to know that by doing that you've declared a revolution! You're not going to wait for us to fix it. You're going to do it! You have the ability and the power to change this nation. And I know you will do it.

"...Allow this to be a rally cry to you to be who you are and to take your place in destiny with a vision.

"God bless you and thank you."

As I sat down, I sensed the warmth and approval of God. I remember wondering at the time how many people had actually heard what I said. We had declared a revolution! Would people take that challenge seriously? Would the youth of America actually take to heart what I sensed the Lord wanted to do in their generation?

I had no way of knowing it then, but at the precise moment that I asked who would take up the torch that had fallen from Rachel's hand, multiplied thousands of young people across the nation jumped from their seats! Around the world, people jumped to their feet and declared their intention to carry Rachel's torch!

In the days following, I began to receive many hundreds of e-mails, cards, letters, and phone calls from people who had heard the call to take up that bloodstained torch! I heard from youth pastors who had taped the broadcast and played that challenge to their youth groups. The reaction was the same everywhere! Hundreds were jumping to their feet and declaring their willingness to carry the torch of Christian witness no matter what the cost! Here are a few typical responses I received. (Many more are included at the back of this book in an addendum.)

Dear Bruce,

Last night in Redmond, Washington, a suburb of Seattle, over 3,000 youth gathered in a city park to "rally" the troops and carry the torch. There were 3 Christian bands performing, and one of the students from Littleton spoke—she called the youth to repent and walk with Christ. It was covered on our local TV station as one of the top 2 stories—Praise the Lord!

The revival is beginning and we are privileged to be a part of it and pray these youth to Christ. Keep up your exciting work—I'm sure there are many stories like mine of our youth rising to the challenge and accepting Rachel's torch. She has accomplished much in her young years for the glory of Jesus Christ. Bless you and your church. I am in awe of how the Lord showed you what was to come.

I believe visions from Him are happening all over the world, and we need only to be open to Him and ask Him what it is we are to do for the Kingdom.

Bless you,
J.K.

Dear Pastor Porter,

I'm a 15-year-old girl from California and am a born-again Christian. I have been so affected by the shootings that I don't even know what to think. I cried and prayed when I heard of the deaths of people so close to my own age, as most of the world was I'm sure.

...I know that tragedies like that of Columbine High School are made for bringing lost souls to God even through the pain. I want you to know that I am right behind you on your quest to carry on the torch and that if there is anything I can do to tell me. I know I am young but I am mature in the ways of the Lord and I want to be his servant!

H.L.

Dear Bruce,

As one who knows nothing about you except what I've received via e-mails, I want to thank you for being willing to take the time to let the world know of the power of God in the lives of these young martyrs at Columbine. The way you worded your thoughts let people like me, a Baptist minister, so far away (Christchurch, New Zealand), know once again the awesomeness of our God as He was able to give strength to these young people in their most terrible moment of need. I suppose it is hard to find the words to truly express what has happened? However, as you put it, we need to find ways for the torch to be handed on to the young people who are now saying they are willing to stand and be counted. I fully agree with your statement, "The killing will not stop with more gun laws, more psychology, more computers in the classrooms, more money for teacher's salaries, etc. Only when there is a change in the hearts of our youth can we hope to stop the slaughter." Could it be that it is time for a concerted effort to reinstate the Bible and prayer in your schools. From the little I know, things have become worse since the abolition of "religion" in schools in the States of the U.S.A. Perhaps I'm speaking out of turn, and with limited knowledge of the system and of the culture—I apologize for my enthusiasm. The Lord bless you as you seek to work a way through this tragedy and to bring hope in the midst of suffering and the bright light of the love of Christ in the midst of the darkness.

I am your fellow traveler,
Kevin Marshall
Pastor, Redwood Baptist Church
Christchurch, New Zealand

*   *   *   *   *

Rachel's funeral was broadcast live and uninterrupted world-wide by CNN. It was later reported to us that this particular event had possibly one of the largest viewing audiences ever recorded in all their broadcast history! I just can't get my mind around that. God did something that all the money in the world couldn't do! He used this terrible act of violence against these children to grab the hearts of people around the entire world!

If the entire body of Christians in the world had given their money to buy all the available airtime on every satellite orbiting the earth and tried to broadcast the gospel, only the tiniest portion of the earth's population would have bothered to watch! As it happened, however, these young martyrs became virtually everyone's children, and the world wept over the tragic loss of their lives. Friends of mine, who were traveling overseas at the time, heard about Rachel's funeral while they were in Singapore! I also received a letter from a family of believers living in Saudi Arabia who related that the funeral was broadcast without censorship on

CNN and BBC. They said that huge numbers of Saudis were glued to their TVs. The Christian gospel was presented to multiplied millions of people around the world in those few short moments. God had certainly done a great miracle!

* * * * *

The following e-mail was sent to me several days after the funeral service for Rachel. As I read it, I could clearly sense the voice of my heavenly Father. May it bless you also.

From: Jim Paul—East Gate Christian Fellowship, Hamilton, Ontario

This is a word the Lord gave me today while watching the funeral of Rachel Joy Scott from Columbine High School. As I watched Rachel's white casket placed at the front of Trinity Christian Center, covered in signatures of mourners, this vision and following word came to me from the Lord.

I saw the casket become very large and it was covered still with signatures—thousands of them this time—but they were prayers for young people. Believers all over the world were interceding for this young generation that is on the brink of burial. All of a sudden an explosion took place and the casket flew open and a whole generation of young people came to life and poured out. A revival of youth is imminent!

This is then what the Lord impressed upon me after the vision was finished:

> *The blood of the martyred teens at Columbine has now been spilt on the ground. Their blood I will now apply to a great breakthrough coming upon the face of the western world. I stood up when Steven's blood was being poured out in Jerusalem by an angry mob. I stood up to honor him (Acts 7), but more than that happened. A young man named Saul filled with rage*

was also standing by watching that murder. He also turned to Me through the events of those days. Steven's blood thrust Paul into My Arms and then into the greatest revival and Apostolic ministry that world had seen.

A revival amongst young people has now been released by this fresh blood of young martyrs. Thousands upon thousands of youth will quickly be saved. Some will rise up in the strength, anointing and the signs of Apostle Paul. The world is about to be shaken by these young Apostles.

Chapter 5

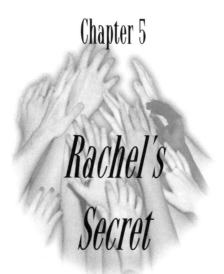

Rachel's Secret

"I am not going to apologize for speaking the name of Jesus,
I am not going to justify my faith to them,
and I am not going to hide the light that God has put into me.
If I have to sacrifice everything...I will. I will take it."
Personal Journal Entry, Rachel Joy Scott, April 20, 1998

The blood of the martyrs is the seed of the church.
Tertullian

After her death, Rachel's family discovered her personal journals. They revealed a deep, secret relationship with Jesus that even her family knew little about. Rachel walked in a depth of relationship with Jesus that displayed a wisdom far beyond her years, and she actually seemed to foreshadow her death in several entries.

One of her personal journals was delayed in being returned to her family for several weeks after her death because it was in her backpack when she died. One of the bullets that passed through her small body was discovered inside her backpack and was considered police evidence until officially released. This bloodstained journal portion is breathtaking in ways you will soon discover.

Rachel surely loved her mother and father very much. Tragically, her family was all too typical of so many broken homes in our times. In her younger years, her dad was a pastor and her family a typical pastor's family. Sadly, in spite of such a nurturing, spiritual family structure, her mother and father tragically divorced more than ten years ago when Rachel was a young child. After the divorce was final, Beth and Darrell had joint custody of the five children, Bethanee, Dana, Rachel, Craig, and Mike.

During those years Beth scrimped and saved, going to school at night while working during the day to support her children. Her son Craig once told me that he would sometimes hear her praying and crying in her bedroom late at night when times were especially hard.

A few days before Mother's Day, just weeks after Rachel's death, Beth was tenderly going through some of her daughter's many writings and drawings. From one of the stacks of papers, a page fell out into Beth's hands. There, in the beautiful script that only Rachel could write, and as a timely gift from a most loving heavenly Father, was the following poem:

SACRIFICE
should be her name,
because she has given up so much for us.

HUMBLE
should be her name,
because she will never admit the great things she has done.

FAITH
should be her name,
because she has enough to carry us, as well as herself,
through this crazy world.

STRENGTH
should be her name,
because she had enough to bear and take care of five children.

WISDOM
should be her name,
because her words and knowledge are worth more than gold.

BEAUTIFUL
should be her name,
because it is not only evident in her face,
but in her heart and soul as well.

GRACEFUL
should be her name,
because she carries herself as a true woman of God.

LOVING
should be her name,
because of the deepness of each hug and kiss she gives us.

ELIZABETH
is her name,
but I call her giving, humble, faithful,
strong, wise, beautiful, graceful, loving mom.

What mother does not yearn to hear such words of tender devotion from her daughter? Rachel has been described by her family as possessing a certain impish joy and uninhibited zeal for life. She would wear funny hats and took joy in wearing clothes that set the pace for fashion as she saw it. Her sisters told me that Rachel once put a message on the family phone recorder that said: "Hello, this is Princess Rachel. Which of her loyal subjects would you like to speak with?" Never at a loss for words, Rachel would say what she thought or felt, and she had a certain refreshing transparency toward everyone. She possessed a highly creative music talent. Her friends spoke of how she would sit at the piano and play the most beautiful music, enrapturing her listeners. When they begged her to play it again, she'd giggle and say she couldn't remember it because she had just made it up!

Once, while performing the mime presentation of "Watch the Lamb" to the music of Ray Boltz to her schoolmates at Columbine, the music suddenly stopped right in the middle of the performance. Well, Rachel just kept dancing! She went faithfully through the motions of her performance while several of her schoolmates chuckled. At last, when the music finally came on again, she was perfectly in sync with it! Everyone was amazed and moved by Rachel's tenacious determination. She won the respect of her classmates that night.

What was ironic about this incident is the fact that the young man who ran the sound system that evening was none other than Dylan Klebold. The music stopped in Rachel's life once, but she kept dancing. The second and final time the music stopped was when Rachel was killed. She is still dancing! No evil or power on earth can stop the heavenly music to which Rachel Joy Scott dances now.

According to everyone who knew her, Rachel wasn't a perfect person. She struggled with some of the same temptations that every other teenager in public high school battles. In spite of this, however, she possessed a quality that was clearly a gift from God. She loved God and was willing to endure isolation, ridicule, and even persecution in order to remain faithful to her Lord Jesus. The eerie thing is, she almost seemed to know that her life would be cut short, and she talked and wrote of that premonition very specifically. In several journal entries she revealed a certain loneliness and abiding sorrow. In an entry dated April 20, 1998, exactly one year to the day before she was martyred, she wrote the following:

"It's like I have a heavy heart and this burden upon my back...but I don't know what it is. There is something in me that makes me want to cry...and I don't even know what it is.

"Things have definitely changed. Last week was so hard...besides missing Breakthru... [a Christian youth ministry she attended] *I lost all of my friends at school. Now that I have begun to 'walk my talk,' they make fun of me. I don't even know what I have done. I don't really have to say anything, and they turn me away. I was talking to ———— and I realized so much. I know what they're thinking every time I make a decision to resist temptation and follow God.*

"They talk behind my back and call me 'the preacher's churchgoing girl...'

"In the last 6 months my friends have changed. There are five of them. We all went to church and were on fire for God. We were close and talked about everything...

"...I have no more personal friends at school. But you know what?...I am not going to apologize for speaking the name of Jesus, I am not going to justify my faith to them, and I am not going to hide the light that God has put into me. If I have to sacrifice everything...I will. I will take it. If my friends have to become my enemies for me to be with my best friend Jesus, then that's fine with me.

45

"Ya know, I always knew that part of being a Christian is having enemies...but I never thought that my 'friends' were going to be those enemies. It's all good, I'm just a loner now at school. I just wish that someone from Breakthru [Christian Ministry] *went to my school.*

"Always in Christ,
"Rachel Joy"

One can sense such loneliness and heartbreak in this journal entry. Rachel made a clear-cut decision to walk with God, and she paid a high price for that fidelity. Her mother learned recently that Rachel even confronted Eric Harris and Dylan Klebold about the dark themes they were celebrating in a photography class a few months before her death. She wasn't mean or rejecting, but lovingly confronted them because they were making films of murder and violence.

Like most people, Rachel struggled sometimes with her faith in God. On March 1, 1998, she wrote these words:

"Dear God, sometimes when I'm craving Your Spirit nothing happens. I stand there with my hands stretched towards heaven crying out Your name, and nothing. Is it because I have not been keeping my quiet times? Is there sin in my life that's keeping me from Your salvation? What can I do? Why have I been able to keep faith like a child until now? Why do I have to question Your existence? I don't understand. I want to feel You."

These questions reveal a gut-level honesty. Rachel, like all of us, sometimes asked hard questions and struggled with her faith in God. She didn't leave it there, though; her next words in this entry also reveal an abiding, powerful undercurrent of confidence and hope.

"I want to feel You in my heart, mind, soul and life. I want heads to turn in the halls when I walk by. I want them to stare at me, watching and wanting the light You've put in me. I want You to overflow my cup with Your Spirit. I want so much from You. I want You to use me to reach the unreached."

*They **are** staring at you, Rachel, watching and wanting that light you had. God is using you now more than you could have possibly imagined while you were here with us.*

Rachel had a heart to reach the world with the gospel of Christ. She was preparing to raise her support for a Teen Mania missions trip to Africa in the summer just before she died. After hearing of Rachel's desire to go to Africa, Evangelist James Robison took Rachel's mom and stepfather with him this past summer to Africa to feed the poor and thereby fulfill part of Rachel's dream.

She concluded the above journal entry with the following cry to God:

"I have such a desire and passion to serve, but I want to do that now. I want to know and serve You now. I want heads to turn now. I want faith like a child now. I want to feel You in my heart, mind and soul now. I want You in my life now. I am crying out to You Father, asking for Your Spirit now. I thank You and love You for all the blessings in my life. Your child, Rachel Joy."

Rachel seemed to have a premonition that her life would be short in this world. There are many evidences for this. For example, one week later on March 8, 1998, she wrote the following entry in her journal:

"God, I have this terrible sharp dull pain in my stomach. I don't know if it's a spiritual feeling. If the enemy is attacking or if it's just sickness. Whatever it is, I ask for Your healing, if it's spiritual feeling I ask for You to bless it, if it's the enemy I ask You to bind it, if it's just sickness I ask You to heal it. Thank You. Rachel Joy."

She talked to several of her friends about this spiritual pain, and after telling her sister Dana, the family became alarmed and had her medically examined. No cause was found physically, but Rachel never shook off the feeling that it was some kind of spiritual occurrence.

Shortly after that she wrote a poem, which read:

"Just passing by
Just coming through
Not staying long
I always knew this home I have will not last."

She actually talked to several of her friends and a cousin and told them that she didn't think she would live very long. She told her cousin one day, "I want to see as much of America as I can before I die." Rachel's dad, Darrell Scott, once said that her sisters told him that even though Rachel was such a beautiful girl, and sometimes expressed an interest in boys, "She never got into wedding dresses. She never talked about those things. Anytime people talked about the future like that, she kind of just got real quiet."

On May 2, 1998, Rachel wrote the following words in her personal journal:

"This will be my last year Lord.
I've gotten what I can.
Thank You."

She couldn't have been writing about her high school because she was only a sophomore in 1998.

Rachel's journals clearly reveal that she believed her time on earth would be brief. Her writings show a young woman fervent in her desire to serve God. Following is the last known entry in her diary.

> *"Am I the only one who sees?*
> *Am I the only one who craves Your glory?*
> *Am I the only one who longs to be forever in Your loving arms?*
> *All I want is for someone to walk with me through*
> *these halls of a tragedy.*
> *Please give me a loving friend who will carry Your name in the end.*
> *Someone who longs to be with You.*
> *Someone who will stay forever true."*

At the Columbine Torchgrab Youth Rally, held in Littleton on August 7, Rachel's 16-year-old brother, Craig, said of his sister:

> "To me, she was just a real person. She was herself and honest and genuine. She was accepting of any person, no matter what they looked like on the outside. She learned

Courtesy of Beth Nimmo

Rachel Joy Scott with her brothers Mike, left, and Craig, right.

to see through that to the person on the inside. I want to be genuine like my sister was. I admire her for that. I just thank God that He's used my sister and answered her prayer to touch so many unreached lives. I just want to challenge the youth today that when you go back to school, to let people see the relationship with God, your personal relationship with God. Let it shine. When kids see that, they want that."

Forty-five minutes before she left this world, a classmate observed Rachel rendering a pencil drawing in her fourth hour class. This drawing, found in her bloodied backpack, was the last she ever drew in this world. It is chilling. Thirteen tears, falling from two disembodied eyes, weeping upon a rose. Only minutes later, 13 people fell, lifeless. Rachel's family believes that the rose represents the youth of America.

Her brother Craig, in an interview in the Denver Post published on October 20, said of this drawing: "I don't think she knew she was drawing it. Was she bored? In the middle of class she just pulls out her journal and draws a picture? If they were writing a Bible today, that would be in it."

Darrell Scott, Rachel's father, made the following observation in an interview with Julia Zaher for Decision Today Radio Magazine, aired August 12, 1999:

"I had a cameraman ask me: 'Where was God when your daughter was killed?' And I just prayed for wisdom in answering. And my answer was: He was at the same place that His Son was at when He was killed 2,000 years ago. But He was also at the same place that my son was at in the library when he was miraculously protected.

"I have no question that God purposed my daughter's life to be taken that day. And that's very hard for people to hear. But I believe that because she was prepared for it.

50

"A year and a half before her death her diaries indicate clearly, not just indicate. She said, I am willing to sacrifice everything to reach the unreached. She said, I'm willing to lay my life down. She quoted the verse, 'Greater love hath no man than this that he lay down his life for his friends.'

"So Rachel's prayer to reach the unreached was answered. It wasn't answered in a way that I would have wanted it to be answered. But sometimes we ask the Father for bread and we get what looks like a stone. We have to bite into that in faith believing that it's going to turn into bread. And that's the path I've chosen. As I've bitten into this tragedy, I've seen it turn into bread.

"I've seen it turn into an evangelistic happening across the world with literally tens of thousands of young people giving their hearts to God. And Rachel would have wanted that. She wouldn't change anything as far as her life is concerned. She would not want me to bring her back and reverse all the good that's happened.

"I think as Christians we all generally agree that God is in control, that He's omniscient, that He's omnipresent, that He's all-powerful, all-knowing. But then when a tragedy occurs we want to excuse Him and we want to basically blame it on guns, or blame it on people, or blame it on the devil. And no one ever sees that God's hand is in the middle of the tragedy as well."

* * * * *

E-mail Update
Wednesday, April 28, 1999

It's therapeutic for me to share my heart with you. So much has happened in the past three days... Thanks to everyone who has written, phoned, e-mailed, and prayed for our community, and for the families and victims. The skies began to clear a little yesterday. It seems that even the heavens have been weeping since last Wednesday.

Rachel's funeral was a supernaturally moving event. Millions of people around the world wept with us as we mourned our losses.

51

There were nearly 3,000 people in attendance as we witnessed so many of her friends share special aspects of her life. It was evident that Rachel's Christian testimony made a major impact on everyone who knew her, and we know it had impact on the people who watched via television as they heard the gospel as reflected in this beautiful young woman's life!

We had an opportunity to challenge the young people present to take the bloodstained torch of God's love in Christ that had fallen from the hand of Rachel and hold it high. When I asked: "Who will take up this torch?" hundreds of young people jumped to their feet and held up their arms to stand with Rachel. It was an electrifying moment. I could sense the tangible presence of God, and the angels seemed to hover over that great crowd as the youths seemed to stand as one person and express their determination to walk as Rachel walked in Christ!

I'm told that at that pivotal moment, young people around the nation jumped to their feet where they were watching and made that pledge. Now we must find ways to help them to do what must be done. With God's help and wisdom, we will know.

The burial service was private. Rachel's casket was placed in a special plot dedicated and donated by the mortuary called: "The Columbine Memorial Garden."

As we gathered around the gravesite, a lone bagpiper played a mournful yet sweet Scottish dirge. All was silent as each of us pastors uttered some word over Rachel. As I rose to speak, I was moved to observe that just as the newly fallen snow covered the ground around us, just so God's amazing grace covers us and makes us pure and white in His sight. That this hallowed ground, broken and scarred by this grave and saddened by the presence of the lifeless body of one so cruelly and unjustly slain, so lovely, so young, so pure, so innocent, would be covered over with such pure white snow so as to make all beneath lovely and pristine. I again felt the holy presence of my Father, and the Holy Spirit. We have sorrow and joy at the same time, for although weeping may endure for a night, joy comes in the morning.

I looked over to Rachel's mother and father. It's so heartbreaking to see a parent bury a child! An ancient proverb states that when a parent buries a child, they bury a part of themselves. Rachel's brothers and sisters wept softly, and it seemed that the angels themselves wept with us as a light rain began to fall. Oh the hope of the resurrection of the dead! How despairing it would be if it were not for the holy promise in the Scriptures that one day, and quite possibly soon, Rachel and every other saint who sleeps in death will arise from the grave!

It now seems credibly evident that the killers were singling out classmates who were believers. Eight of the 12 students killed were known for their strong faith. The consistency of their question, "Do you believe in God?" in the case of Valeen Schnurr, and quite likely, Cassie Bernall, gives reason that in all likelihood, Rachel Scott was also confronted in a similar way.

We know that Rachel was sitting outside the cafeteria with Richard Castaldo. As the killers approached, they sprayed Rachel and Richard with a hail of bullets. Rachel was hit in the leg, arm, and chest. Richard tried to flee, and was shot nine times before he fell. He miraculously survived, although paralyzed. There is an unsubstantiated rumor circulating that Harris then reached down, grabbed Rachel by her hair, and shouted, "Do you still believe in your God now?" She answered, "You know that I do." He reportedly replied, "Then go and be with Him now!" Putting the gun to her temple, he fired. She died instantly.

Today, the exact day one week ago that these students were killed or injured, I visited Rachel's family home and prayed with them. Pastor Dutch Sheets also came over that morning to join us in prayer. Dutch shared some words of encouragement with Beth and Larry that were tender and anointed. All of us could sense the sweet presence of the Lord in that home as we sought the comfort of our heavenly Father. As we were praying together, at exactly the same moment the massacre occurred last week, all radio and television stations across Denver went silent for one minute. The faint sounds of church bells could be heard across Littleton, as they tolled mournfully, and people stopped what they were doing and remembered.

The sun finally came out today. It's been cloudy and cold ever since the massacre. Maybe we're all beginning to heal a little. I still cry at odd times. Most of us do it seems. Funerals are going on all week as we try to bury our children and pick up the pieces once again. Rachel and the other slain children have become everyone's children. As we mourn together, we learn anew the preciousness of life, and how easily it can slip away.

Out of this disaster, we are witnessing an amazing opening of the hearts of people to the things of God. We've seen more people turn to Jesus in the past week than we've ever seen. God is doing something that is spreading all over the nation.

Tomorrow I am off to Virginia Beach to be a guest on CBN's 700 Club on Thursday morning. Please pray for me that I will be supernaturally enabled to faithfully represent our community to the nation's Christians. More than this, pray that I will be able to inspire the viewers to "take up the torch" that fell from the hands of Rachel and Cassie. I'm praying that these deaths will be the pivotal point in a new and fresh move of God among our nation's youth. Please join me. The killing will not stop with more gun laws, more psychology, more computers in the classrooms, more money for teacher's salaries, etc. Only when there is a change in the hearts of our youth can we hope to stop the slaughter. Jesus can make that difference, and we can encourage and embolden the youth of America to stand up and demand safer schools by confronting evil in their midst.

It's nearly 1:30 a.m. and I have to get up in a few hours and catch a plane. Goodnight and I love you.

Pastor Bruce Porter

Perhaps Rachel and John greeted each other as they grabbed their backpacks and walked together across the park toward the school...and into history.

Chapter 6

A National Emergency!

"I'm drowning—in my own lake of despair.
I'm choking—my hands wrapped around my neck.
I'm dying—quickly my soul leaves
slowly my body withers.

"It isn't suicide, I consider it homicide.
The world you have created
has led to my death..."

Rachel Joy Scott

The late morning of April 20 found Eric Harris and Dylan Klebold waiting in the school parking lot just outside the Columbine High School cafeteria. Waiting was something Eric and Dylan had long practiced over the past year, and they were undoubtedly becoming quite good at it. For nearly a year they had conspired, planned, plotted, observed school schedules and student movements, and worked diligently to amass a formidable arsenal of pipe bombs, firearms, and a very large propane tank bomb.

> As they sat outside, watching students coming in and out of the building, the timers on the detonators of the bombs containing two 20-pound bottles of propane were ticking, ticking, ticking. Eric and Dylan waited, expecting their diabolical invention to soon unleash a huge explosion and fireball of hell's fury, burning alive more than 600 of their fellow students at precisely 11:15 a.m. They had carefully calculated this to be the exact time when the maximum number of students would be in the cafeteria.

It's quite likely that as the moment of detonation drew near, they counted it down, enjoying each second's march toward what they hoped would be the unleashing of their monstrous holocaust. Five, four, three, two, one...and then, nothing happened. Perhaps they sat in dazed amazement as the scene before them failed to disintegrate into a hellish ball of flame, terrified screams, and burning flesh. The birds were still singing, the students continued to laugh and talk inside and outside the cafeteria in the warm spring sunshine, and...nothing happened.

Perhaps they flew into a rage when they realized that their "weapon of first choice" had failed them. Now they had to fall back on a secondary plan of action. Their orgy of blood would now have to be up close and personal. Jumping from the car, they strapped on their weapons, ammunition, and pipe bombs. After arming the booby traps previously installed on their cars—apparently in the hope that after their orgy of bloodshed had concluded a police officer or firefighter would be maimed or killed when investigating their vehicles—Eric and Dylan pulled on their trench coats to conceal their weapons and began walking toward the school.

Some of the students outside probably saw them coming, but paid little attention until it was too late.

I recently talked with a CBI (Colorado Bureau of Investigation) officer who was on the scene at Columbine shortly after the massacre. I asked him why the propane bomb in the cafeteria had not exploded. He told me it had failed because of a single faulty strand of wire in the detonator. One single wire! I asked the officer if the bomb was otherwise functional would have exploded if it were not for that single defect. He looked me square in the eye and said, "Those kids in the cafeteria were incredibly lucky!" I responded that quite likely the grace of God prevented what might have been the single most monstrous crime in American history!

According to investigators, had those bombs detonated, every one of the 660 kids in the cafeteria would have suffered a death more horrible than the human mind can fathom. Nearly four times the number of people who died in the Oklahoma City bombing would have perished!

In light of the above, we must ask ourselves why some are harping so single-mindedly on the gun issue. It should be clear to everyone by now that Eric and Dylan's "weapon of first choice" wasn't firearms at all! If those bombs had detonated, we would most likely be having a much different public debate.

I feel like I'm only now coming up for air. I fight depression sometimes. It's more than the experience of witnessing up close and personal a tragedy of such huge proportions. Rather, I feel like I've been assaulted by an incessant barrage of mind-numbing banalities and vain repetitions of humanistic clichés offered by secular pundits, opportunistic politicians, and not a few religious leaders who should know better. The solutions thus far offered to stem the violence in our schools by those presently in authority in the school systems are a comedy of errors. Far from being a comedy, however, the inevitable outcome of their ideas will, without any doubt in my mind, doom us to repeat performances of what we witnessed at Columbine.

> *For they have healed the hurt of the daughter of My people slightly, saying, "Peace, peace!" when there is no peace* (Jeremiah 8:11 NKJV).

The lessons of Columbine are spiritual. It now seems crystal clear that in the past four decades, our nation's moral fabric has been systematically shredded, leaving us with an enormous population of people who are essentially amoral. Relativism and revisionist history in our nation's primary and secondary schools have turned out people who not only can't read and write, but who also have no sense of honor or awareness of cultural continuity.

We are constantly being told that people would be civil if we would only be "tolerant" of each person in their diversity. This is a very noble and lofty ideal, but in actual practice, tolerance has now become a politically correct cliché used to silence anyone who dares call evil, evil. Suppose that my personal expression of diversity included the belief that it's okay to blow up schools full of students and teachers? Should society be expected to be "tolerant" of such ideas, let alone the expression of them? And yet, that evil, twisted concept of "tolerance" was the very thing that paralyzed teachers, school administrators, and even the police from doing anything to prevent this disaster!

When Eric Harris and Dylan Klebold produced a film project at Columbine that virtually depicted what they intended to actually *do*, hardly anyone questioned them. Harris wrote on his website, before AOL took it down, "I don't care if I live or die in the shootout. All I want to do is kill and injure as many of you f——s as I can."[1] He and Klebold even modified the vicious video game DOOM so that the layout of the game resembled Columbine High School's floor plan. The police revealed that Harris' personal diary was full of Nazi phrases in German, and it revealed a year's worth of careful planning for the attack to take place on Hitler's birthday. Harris drew detailed maps of the school showing hiding places, as well as where and when the most students would be. One family, whose son was threatened by Harris, tried to get the Jefferson County Sheriff's Department to intervene after downloading dozens of pages of Harris' website in which he threatened to kill everyone he didn't like. Incredibly, the authorities ignored this family's concerns and did nothing whatsoever!

Every form of sexual perversion, artistic debauchery, gross behavior, filthy speech, and violent entertainment has become the equivalent of a "protected species" under the rubric of "tolerance." At the same time, however, those who would raise objection to certain behaviors on the basis of biblical standards are often vilified as hate mongers and moralistic bigots!

Where is our sense of moral outrage? Our people have become desensitized to violence and debauchery, largely through the trivializing of the grossest forms of human behavior in the entertainment establishment. Consider, for example, the following quote by popular "shock jock" Howard Stern spoken a few days after the Columbine carnage.

> "There were some really good-looking girls running out with their hands over their heads. Did those kids [Harris and Klebold] try to have sex with any of the good-looking girls? They didn't even do that? At least if you're going to kill yourself and kill all the kids, why wouldn't you have some sex? If I was going to kill some people, I would take 'em out with some sex."

Do you grasp what Stern just said? For anyone to advocate the idea that Harris and Klebold should have added the outrage of rape to their rampage of terror is beyond all boundaries of human decency! Can we even faintly imagine how this statement must have traumatized and devastated the family and friends of the slain young women? Should the courtesy of "tolerance" be extended to such brutish speech? The fact that Stern is yet broadcasting and

61

attracting sponsors is clear testimony that utter outrage over such unspeakable profanation in our society is yet to be awakened.

The value of human life has been cheapened in our nation. A prime example is the widely accepted practice of murdering children in their mother's womb. Fully one-third of this present generation of young people has already been slaughtered by their own mothers! This holocaust has become even more horrific as the boundaries of "acceptable" practice in the child extermination industry now allow for the child to be nearly born except for his head (so he can't scream) and for shoving a pair of scissors into the back of the baby's head so his brain can be sucked out. A new twist to this macabre practice is the establishment of organ harvesting businesses adjacent to these murder mills, which take the organs of these freshly slaughtered children and make fortunes!

The old story of the frog in the kettle is applicable. As the heat slowly rises, the frog is not alarmed and slowly cooks to death, whereas if the frog were thrown suddenly into hot water he would quickly and easily jump out. I fear that our collective frog may already be cooked.

In our nation we have recently endured many, many shocking incidents of school violence where innocent children and teachers have been killed or wounded. Here is a list of them...thus far...

January 18, 1993: Grayson, Kentucky: Two killed.
February 1, 1993: Amityville, New York: One killed, one wounded.
October 12, 1995: Blackville, South Carolina: Two killed, one wounded.
October 23, 1995: Redlands, California: One killed, one wounded.
November 15, 1995: Lynnville, Tennessee: Two killed, one wounded.
February 2, 1996: Moses Lake, Washington: Three killed, one wounded.

62

February 19, 1997: Bethel, Alaska: One killed.

October 1, 1997: Pearl (Jackson), Mississippi: Two killed, seven wounded.

December 1, 1997: Paducah, Kentucky: Three killed, five wounded.

December 15, 1997: Stamps, Arkansas: Two wounded.

March 24, 1998: Jonesboro, Arkansas: Five killed, ten wounded.

April 24, 1998: Edinboro, Pennsylvania: One killed, three wounded.

May 21, 1998: Springfield, Oregon: Four killed, twenty wounded.

June 15, 1998: Richmond, Virginia: Two wounded.

April 20, 1999: Littleton, Colorado: Thirteen killed, twenty-three wounded.

April 28, 1999: Taber, Alberta, Canada: One killed, one wounded.

May 20, 1999: Conyers, Georgia: Six wounded.

And now, even beyond the carnage in the schools listed above, we are seeing vicious attacks by crazed madmen against small children in daycare centers and schoolyards. Most recently, we have beheld the outrage of the killings at a youth gathering in a church in Fort Worth, Texas.

September 15, 1999: Fort Worth, Texas, Wedgwood Baptist Church: Seven killed, seven wounded.

Our popular culture has long forsaken the foundational principles upon which our nation was established in its infancy and wandered off into a fog of narcissistic hedonism. The mere mention of biblical morality and its applicability in our nation's public schools is met with derision and recitations of the popular secular mantra: "separation of church and state." People of good conscience, who acknowledge that God is the ultimate authority regarding what is good and evil, right and wrong, have allowed themselves to be intimidated into silence by those who would undermine and destroy any remaining vestige of our once proud Judeo-Christian heritage. The fruit of this slide into amoral oblivion is now lying in caskets, buried in cemeteries across our nation, with the grass growing on these fresh graves watered by the tears of brokenhearted parents.

The following speech was given by Rachel's father, Darrell Scott, before the Subcommittee on Crime, House Judiciary Committee, in Washington, D.C., on Thursday, May 27, 1999.

"Since the dawn of creation there has been both good and evil in the heart of men and of women. We all contain the seeds of kindness or the seeds of violence.

"The death of my wonderful daughter Rachel Joy Scott, and the deaths of that heroic teacher and the other children who died must not be in vain. Their blood cries out for answers.

"The first recorded act of violence was when Cain slew his brother Abel out in the field. The villain was not the club he used. Neither was it the NCA, the National Club Association. The true killer was Cain and the reason for the murder could only be found in Cain's heart.

"In the days that followed the Columbine tragedy, I was amazed at how quickly fingers began to be pointed at groups such as the NRA. I am not a member of the NRA. I am not a hunter. I do not even own a gun. I am not here to represent or defend the NRA—because I don't believe that they are responsible for my daughter's death. Therefore I do not believe that they need to be defended. If I believed they had anything to do with Rachel's murder I would be their strongest opponent.

"I am here today to declare that Columbine was not just a tragedy—it was a spiritual event that should be forcing us to look at where the real blame lies! Much of that blame lies here in this room. Much of that blame lies behind the pointing fingers of the accusers themselves...

"I wrote a poem just four nights ago that express my feelings best. This was written way before I knew I would be speaking here today.

> Your laws ignore our deepest needs
> Your words are empty air.
> You've stripped away our heritage.
> You've outlawed simple prayer.
>
> Now gunshots fill our classrooms.
> And precious children die.
> You seek for answers everywhere.
> And ask the question "WHY"?
>
> You regulate restrictive laws.
> Through legislative creed.
> And yet you fail to understand.
> That God is what we need!

"Men and women are three-part beings. We all consist of body, soul, and spirit. When we refuse to acknowledge a third part of our make-up, we create a void that allows evil, prejudice, and hatred to rush in and wreak havoc. Spiritual influences were present within our educational systems for most of our nation's history. Many of our major colleges began as theological seminaries. This is a historic fact.

"What has happened to us as a nation? We have refused to honor God and in doing so, we open the doors to hatred and violence. And when something as terrible as Columbine's tragedy occurs—politicians immediately look for a scapegoat such as the NRA. They immediately seek to pass more restrictive laws that continue to erode away our personal and private liberties.

"We do not need more restrictive laws. Eric and Dylan would not have been stopped by metal detectors. No amount of gun laws can stop someone who spends months planning this type of massacre. The real villain lies within our OWN hearts. Political posturing and restrictive legislation [are] not the answers.

"The young people of our nation hold the key. There is a spiritual awakening taking place that will not be squelched!

"We do not need more religion. We do not need more gaudy television evangelists spewing out verbal religious garbage. We do not need more million dollar church buildings built while people with basic needs are being ignored. We do need a change of heart and an humble acknowledgment that this nation was founded on the principle of simple trust in God.

"As my son Craig lay under that table in the school library, and saw his two friends murdered before his very eyes, he did not hesitate to pray in school. I defy any law or politician to deny him that right! I challenge every young person in America and around the world to realize that on April 20, 1999, at Columbine High School—prayer was brought back to our schools. Do not let the many prayers offered by those students be in vain. Dare to move into the new millennium with a sacred disregard for legislation that violates your conscience and denies your God-given right to communicate with Him.

"To those of you who would point your finger at the NRA—I give to you a sincere challenge. Dare to examine your own heart before you cast the first stone! My daughter's death will not be in vain. The young people of this country will not allow that to happen."

* * * * *

Rachel's words, penned in her personal journal shortly before April 20, 1999, continue to haunt me.

"The world you have created has led to my death..."

She may not have been aware of the spiritual warfare taking place in the unseen realm, but Rachel certainly understood the struggle that a committed Christian endures in our nation's public schools. She walked in a hostile environment where her faith in Christ was alien to the predominate culture. Eric and Dylan shared a photography class with Rachel, where they were engaged in the creation of film projects that elevated the theme of killing their teachers and fellow students! Why didn't someone confront them about that? Rachel did. According to eyewitnesses, she lovingly confronted Harris, and then, on April 20, she was killed.

Was she targeted because she was a Christian? It's now an established fact. In a home video created on March 15, 1999, Harris and Klebold seethed with hatred toward born-again Christians, and Rachel in particular. Her name is mentioned twice in their tirades. Following is a transcript of a portion of one of those videos. I caution you that the explicit language is offensive...

Eric: "Shut the f—— up Nick—you laugh too much. And those girls sitting next to you, they probably want you to shut up too. Rachel and Jen and whatever."

Dylan: "Stuck up little b———, you f—— little Christianity, godly wh—!"

Eric: "Yeh, (mockingly) 'I love Jesus, I love Jesus,' shut the f—— up!"

Dylan: (mockingly) "What would Jesus do?" (makes a face at the camera and then yells) "What would I do? Booosh!" (points at camera [as if holding] a shotgun)

Eric: "I would shoot you in the m———— f———head! Go Romans— Thank God they crucified that A—— H——!!"

Both: "Go Romans! Go Romans! Yea! Whoooh!"[2]

It is beyond question that Rachel was killed because of her witness for Christ. To those who might yet try to discredit this assertion in light of the above empirical proof, I can only say that your failure to see the plain truth of this fact is willful denial. Rachel was counted worthy to suffer a martyr's death, and her spilled blood cries out from the earth!

E-mail Update
May, 1999

I've sat down so many times and tried to write, but it was just too painful. Part of me wants to somehow forget what has happened here, and yet, my heart tells me that pain can often serve as a volume knob so we can more clearly discern the voice of God.

The time of ministry with the 700 Club in Virginia Beach was refreshing. The sweet saints there were so very gracious and sensitive. I truly felt reinvigorated after being among them, even though the schedule was tight. I was afforded the distinct honor of addressing the CBN staff in their chapel service after the interviews, and there was such a sweet presence of the Lord there in the worship and fellowship. I pray that my humble remarks served to strengthen and encourage them in the amazing ministry God has raised up among them.

When I flew home to Denver later that night, I drove directly from the airport to the memorials set up in the park adjacent to Columbine H.S. I was so tired, but I wanted to spend some quiet time there to collect my thoughts. As I stood before Rachel's car, covered over with so many flowers and cards that one could scarcely discern the automobile underneath, it began to rain heavily. I couldn't move. Such a sense of grief and sorrow overcame me that I just stood there in the pouring rain weeping, mingling my tears with those of so many others.

That's when I became angry. I became angry that this slaughter of the innocents had occurred in MY town, down the street from MY church, and on MY watch. I felt angry at a society seemingly gone mad, glorifying filth and violence and selfish indifference. Angry at myself for being so self-absorbed in the past, not wanting to see the warning signals, and seeking comfort zones in denial instead of caring more. I was angry at the devil for using the opportunities we all granted him through our selfish preoccupation to destroy our youth and lay waste our people.

I remain angry; however, it's not simply an emotion of anger, no, but rather more like a rising sense of determined conviction that I must DO SOMETHING. Columbine H.S. has become synonymous in my mind with a sort of spiritual PEARL HARBOR event! I am convinced that millions of others are feeling the same way.

These young people of Columbine, who shed their blood and lives at the hands of what can only be described as demon-possessed maniacs, have left us a precious gift. It is a gift of COURAGE. Courage to stand up for what is right, true, and just!

Pastor Bruce Porter

Endnotes

1. Rocky Mountain News, 4-30-99 pg. 4A.

2. A copy of this transcript was handed to all the attendees (including the author) at the December 20, 1999, press conference held by Darrell Scott at Trinity Christian Center in Littleton, Colorado.

Chapter 7

Retaking Our Schools
. . . Retaking Our Nation

In mid-August I attended the opening rally at Columbine High School. The day dawned crisply, with the hint of fall in the air. My good friend Steve Wichael, a leader in our church, accompanied me that morning as we walked the long distance from the last available parking spaces over half a mile from the school. Literally thousands of people came that morning from all over the community, including the multitudes of media people who came to cover this "Retaking Our School" event. The eyes of the world were on Columbine once again, only this time, instead of watching terror and anguish, they would feast on scenes of thousands gathered in the school parking lot celebrating the reopening of Columbine.

Steve had attended and graduated from Columbine High School some years ago, and he appeared to be deeply in thought as we walked. I wandered absentmindedly among the crowd, listening to the hyped announcements from the platform and the upbeat rock 'n' roll blasting from the huge PA system. Student cheerleaders were dancing on the platform, giving a sense that a rock festival was taking place.

In order to gain a better view of the stage, Steve and I walked up the steps outside the ill-fated school library where most of the carnage took place and watched the scene below unfold. At one point someone on the platform called for a pledge of allegiance to the flag. I raised my hand to my heart in salute to our nation's flag, as did many of the people around me, including several police officers. As the pledge was recited, I looked all around me in vain for a glimpse of Old Glory. It was nowhere to be seen! From my vantage point I could see all the grounds, and it quickly became apparent that no one had thought to display the very object of our pledge! The officer standing next to me glanced over and commented that this was really strange!

Suddenly, a terrible realization came over me. We were standing just outside the cafeteria—very nearly over the spot where Rachel had fallen and died! A feeling of nausea came over me! There was no marker, no memorial, no outward indication that anything out of the ordinary had occurred there, but the feeling I got at that moment was indescribable. I looked a few feet further up the sidewalk and recognized the spot where Dan Rohrbaugh had fallen and where students had run panic-stricken past his lifeless body in their effort to escape the library. The entire scene began to feel macabre.

Steve and I walked down toward the platform. As we drew nearer, one of the student body leaders was giving a pep talk on how, in spite of all the broken windows in the school, one particular window remained untouched. It was the one with the "Rebel Man" school mascot, and he opined that there was some strange significance to this. He never directly referred to the slaughter that took place mere weeks ago, and he avoided any mention of the dead or wounded.

Nor did anyone else on the platform mention the tragedy in any direct way. Not once did anyone speak of those who died or of the suffering of the wounded! Looking around at the crowd, who seemed completely oblivious to what was happening, I searched for any victim family members, wondering how they might be reacting to this glaring omission. I looked back at the stage just as one of the coaches began to lead the crowd in a cheer. The coach began screaming over and over into the blaring microphone, "We are...!" as some of the crowd shouted back, "Columbine!" This went on and on and on! Looking around again at the uncomprehending faces around me as they maniacally chanted, I was reminded of some ancient film footage of the crowds of Red Guards in China who would chant Mao's slogans until they worked themselves into a frenzy, while Chairman Mao looked on smirking. The whole scene was bizarre! The expression on hundreds of young faces was nothing short of catatonic.

I came very close to making a scene. I thought of shouting up to the platform, "Can we please have a minute of silence for those who died?" This breach of simple human decency was almost overwhelming in its impact. Only after the rally did we learn of how utterly devastated the victim family members who were in attendance felt. Their children, whose lives were so brutally terminated just a few months before, didn't even merit a single mention of their names! It was in such poor taste to not even give a few moments of recognition to those families or their children, who would never walk the halls of that school again.

I realize that the leaders of the "Retaking Our School" rally were attempting to impart a sense of hope and new beginnings. They wanted to help the students overcome any fears that they might have of returning to the classroom and give them a feeling of normalcy and school spirit. To their credit, the school authorities were trying to make the day as bright as possible, but I came away from the rally feeling a shadow of darkness.

So, at this point someone will say, "Okay, what solution do you propose to this 'National Emergency'? What recommendations do you offer for 'Retaking Our Schools'?"

> *Therefore I exhort first of all that supplications, prayers, intercessions, and giving of thanks be made for all men, for kings and all who are in authority, that we may lead a quiet and peaceable life in all godliness and reverence. For this is good and acceptable in the sight of God our Savior, who desires all men to be saved and to come to the knowledge of the truth* (1 Timothy 2:1-4 NKJV)

I am completely convinced that if we do not pray for our leaders, then we are doomed to see the tragedy at Columbine repeated over and over again across our nation. How desperately our public officials and politicians need our prayers! If we hope to change things, we cannot do it by angry confrontation. That will accomplish nothing. I know that in my own emotional anguish and "righteous indignation" during the "back to school" rally, I was tempted to take matters into my own hands. I'm so thankful that in those moments my spiritual sense overcame my natural and common sense! We must do battle at a higher level! It is the Lord who can reach the hearts of the leaders of this country, set them free from the fog of confusion, and help them to make wise decisions. It is only the Lord who can open their eyes to the real nature and source of the assault raging against this generation.

When I read Psalm 64 at Rachel's funeral, I was struck by the amazing parallels between what the psalmist was describing and what happened at Columbine High School that fateful day: "They shoot from ambush at the innocent, attacking suddenly and fearlessly."[1]

The first rule of effective warfare is to know your enemy. The people who contend with us, who persecute, abuse, and even murder our brothers and sisters in Christ, are not really our problem! Our real enemies are unseen evil forces who deceive, manipulate, and use people who are unsuspectingly enslaved. Our chief aim and purpose is to pray and intercede for people who are captive, that they might come into the light of truth and liberty.

The well-meaning solutions offered by the Jefferson County School Board to prevent another tragedy, for the most part, fall short of what is actually and so desperately needed. Natural weapons are not, and cannot be, effective in a spiritual war. My mind reels under the weight of the banality of ideas like each student wearing an "ID badge," or the installation of more surveillance cameras, or the institution of a "snitch hotline" with which students could anonymously call in reports of suspicious behaviors by fellow students. Eric and Dylan might have worn their "ID badges" into school that fateful day, and the surveillance cameras might have caught their images in 70mm Imax color, but they wouldn't have made any difference regarding the outcome. The existing cameras dutifully recorded their rampage even as their victims begged for mercy! As for "snitching," the facts bear out that several students complained of being threatened by Eric Harris, and one family tried to get the authorities to intervene after their son received death threats from Harris. They printed out huge portions of Harris' rantings from his website and gave them to the police, who chose to do nothing whatsoever about it.

Oh yes, and what of the clamor for "gun control" by those looking for quick, politically correct fixes? The fear and hysteria whipped up by anti-gun activists against the National Rifle Association was simply another exercise in "straw man" blame shifting. The fact is, the role of firearms in the Columbine massacre is now clearly established as Harris and Klebold's secondary choice of weapons! What the media has virtually ignored in their anti-gun frenzy and what the general public seems only mildly interested in, is the fact that Harris and Klebold fully intended to burn alive more than 500 students with their propane bomb! They very nearly succeeded!

We all can be somewhat comforted that, by the grace of God, the propane bomb didn't detonate. If it had, I suspect we would not be hearing nearly as much about banning firearm ownership as we are. Perhaps we'd be holding hearings on banning "assault propane tanks." "More laws!" some would cry. "We need more laws to prevent another Columbine!" The last time I checked, Harris and Klebold disregarded with impunity more than 19 separate state and federal laws in their suicide mission. If laws could have saved Rachel and the other killed and wounded people at Columbine, then April 20 would have been a non-event. The only law able to prevent another Columbine is the *law of God* being raised to its rightful place as a standard in our nation. We must recognize that the fight we are in is a spiritual battle and that it will be won only by using spiritual weapons and tools.

> *For we are not fighting against people made of flesh and blood, but against the evil rulers and authorities of the unseen world, against those mighty powers of darkness who rule this world, and against wicked spirits in the heavenly realms* (Ephesians 6:12).

Prior to 1962 the majority of crimes in our schools consisted of things like smoking in the bathroom or throwing spit wads in class. Now, all too frequently, the crimes are robbery, rape, assaults on students and teachers, and more recently, mass murder. The one defining event that has taken place in our nation is the removal of prayer from our public schools by judicial fiat in June of 1962. The object of the court's deliberation, the nefarious prayer that became the subject of such loathing by well-meaning secular humanists, was simply this: "*Almighty God, we acknowledge our dependence upon Thee, and we beseech Thy blessing on us, our parents, our teachers, and our country.*"

Prayer, or the lack thereof, has been the defining factor! The restraining force that reduced the influence of evil and confusion in this broken and fallen world was diminished, and the forces of darkness have filled the vacuum!

What is the answer? More protests? More parents angrily confronting school boards? More lawsuits against public servants? No. None of these will prevail. God has placed a much more powerful weapon in our arsenal.

Love.

Love? A weapon? Most definitely! When used against the forces of darkness that blind people's minds, love is the equivalent to a nuclear bomb!

> We must not confront this culture and the sin of our people with the rhetoric of anger or self-righteous condemnation.

We must not confront this culture and the sin of our people with the rhetoric of anger or self-righteous condemnation, but with prayer, intercession, and a broken and contrite heart. Jesus never railed at sinners, nor did He condemn people who were ensnared by sin in all its myriad forms. He saved His most scathing condemnation for those self-righteous religious bigots who fancied themselves better than everyone else and who wore their piety as a badge of superiority. When we talk of sin and depravity in the lives of people who are enslaved to it, we should do so with tears in our eyes and compassion in our hearts! We must always remember that God is able to turn Sauls into Pauls!

We are all, each and every one of us, desperately in need of a Savior. Those of us who are more aware of our need ought not to smugly condemn those who have yet to awaken to it, and we should never speak of another's sin without mist in our eyes.

I think about the lesson of the prophet Jonah and the wicked city of Nineveh in the Bible. Most people, when reading this portion of Scripture, key in on the giant fish that swallowed Jonah, usually as a way of ridiculing or discrediting the entire account. However, the fish is not the central theme of this portion of Scripture.

77

The Lord gave this message to Jonah son of Amittai: "Get up and go to the great city of Nineveh! Announce My judgment against it because I have seen how wicked its people are." But Jonah got up and went in the opposite direction in order to get away from the Lord. He went down to the seacoast, to the port of Joppa, where he found a ship leaving for Tarshish. He bought a ticket and went on board, hoping that by going away to the west he could escape from the Lord (Jonah 1:1-3).

Have you ever wondered why Jonah tried to run away from the Lord and not deliver God's message of warning to this wicked city? Some have tried to say that Jonah was afraid of the Ninevites because they were famous for their cruelties against the Hebrews. The evil Ninevites would tie people to wagon wheels and drive around the city while the bodies of their hapless victims were beaten to pulp by the city cobblestones. That was only one of the milder things they would do.

I do not think that Jonah's response was rooted in fear. Jonah knew that the fact that God was even bothering to deliver a warning to the Ninevites meant that they could possibly repent and be forgiven! Jonah simply *didn't want them to be forgiven!* He *wanted* the wrath of God to fall on these evildoers because of all the havoc they had caused His people! I wonder if this is not the same attitude of many of God's followers today?

When Jonah finally got his navigation and obedience sorted out—through God's submarine provision—he did go to Nineveh and warn the people. Jonah probably spoke his message hoping all the while that no one would pay any attention to him!

This time Jonah obeyed the Lord's command and went to Nineveh, a city so large that it took three days to see it all. On the day Jonah entered the city, he shouted to the crowds: "Forty days from now Nineveh will be destroyed!" The people of Nineveh believed God's message, and from the greatest to the least, they decided to go without food and wear sackcloth to show their sorrow. When the king of Nineveh heard what Jonah was saying, he stepped down from his throne and took off his royal robes. He dressed himself in sackcloth and sat on a heap of ashes. Then the king and his nobles sent this decree throughout the city: "No one, not even the animals, may eat or drink anything at all. Everyone is required to wear sackcloth and pray earnestly to God. Everyone must turn from their evil ways and stop all their violence. Who can tell? Perhaps even yet God will have pity on us and hold back His fierce anger from destroying us." When God saw that they had put a stop to their evil ways, He had mercy on them and didn't carry out the destruction He had threatened (Jonah 3:3-10).

This portion of Scripture was included in our Bibles for a divine reason! God reserves for Himself the right to move upon the hearts of anyone He chooses to bring forth the fruit of repentance! This huge city, with hundreds of thousands of people, groped for God and found Him. They sincerely responded to the move of God's Spirit and repented, and God had mercy upon them! Notice what Jonah's attitude was when he beheld the mercy of God toward Nineveh:

This change of plans upset Jonah, and he became very angry. So he complained to the Lord about it: "Didn't I say before I left home that You would do this, Lord? That is why I ran away to Tarshish! I knew that You were a gracious and compassionate God, slow to get angry and filled with unfailing love. I knew how easily You could cancel Your plans for destroying these people" (Jonah 4:1-2).

Now, let us compare our hearts to Jonah's when we regard our own nation. The sins of the United States of America have piled high. We have become a nation full of violence, hatred, greed, murder, robbery, sexual perversion, and arrogant pride. Our once proud heritage of moral rectitude, envisioned by those early believers who came to this nation as pilgrims and finally embodied in our amazing Constitution, has now crumbled into a dim memory. We now export our shame in the form of pornography, violent entertainment, and highly efficient weapons for the oppressors of this world to murder their own people.

The cup of our collective shame is nearly full, and an unspeakable judgment is at our very door. Our only hope is repentance as a people. Are God's people settling back in seats of judgment, calling for God's punishment to fall, or are we calling upon His mercy and forgiveness? Are we declaring His Word with anointing and authority, raising it as the standard of truth for all to see?

Most Americans are completely unaware that the Declaration of Independence came into being only after a day of fasting and prayer had been observed. The day was declared by the Continental Congress, and it was observed by all the colonies on May 17, 1776. At that time in our history, our people honored God and the Bible much more than they do today. When our nation was finally born, our forefathers rang the Liberty Bell with such joy and enthusiasm that a legend says that it cracked as they zealously proclaimed their freedom. Some years later the White Chapel Foundry of London offered to recast the huge bell, but their proposal was politely refused. Apparently the symbolic value of the damaged bell, which recalls the religious and patriotic fervor of those early days, was something that early Americans wanted to preserve.

But in light of our nation's moral decline, the crack could also suggest a break in our foundational ideals and a serious defect in our spiritual health. We can remedy the situation and avert judgment only by repentance, prayer, and a return to the faith of our ancestors. Considering the clear and present danger we face, there is no time for delay in "mending the bell."

* * * * *

...that you may become blameless and pure, children of God without fault in a crooked and depraved generation, in which you shine like stars in the universe as you hold out the word of life... (Philippians 2:15-16 NIV).

80

On November 30, 1998, Senior Pastor Joe Wright of the Central Christian Church in Topeka, Kansas, was asked to open the new session of the Kansas Senate in prayer. Everyone was expecting the usual religious pabulum, but Joe was obviously connected to a higher wattage spiritual circuit that day.

The response was far from insignificant. Several legislators angrily stormed out during the prayer in protest. In a few short weeks, Pastor Wright's church logged more than 5,000 phone calls, with only 47 responding negatively. Requests for copies of the prayer came from India, Africa, and Korea. Paul Harvey aired the prayer on "The Rest of the Story" program and received a larger response to this program than any other to date.

This prayer summarizes the essence of the responsibility set before us as Christians to pray for our nation and leaders:

"Heavenly Father, we come before You today to ask Your forgiveness and to seek Your direction and guidance. We know Your Word says, 'Woe on those who call evil good,' but that's exactly what we have done. We have lost our spiritual equilibrium and reversed our values. We confess that:

- We have ridiculed the absolute truth of Your Word and called it pluralism.

- We have worshiped other gods and called it multi-culturalism.

- We have endorsed perversion and called it an alternative lifestyle.

- We have exploited the poor and called it the lottery.

- We have neglected the needy and called it self-preservation.

- We have rewarded laziness and called it welfare.

- We have killed our unborn children and called it a choice.

- We have shot abortionists and called it justifiable.

- We have neglected to discipline our children and called it building self-esteem.

- We have abused power and called it political savvy.

- We have coveted our neighbor's possessions and called it ambition.

- We have polluted the air with profanity and pornography and called it freedom of expression.

- We have ridiculed the time-honored values of our forefathers and called it enlightenment.

"Search us, O God, and know our hearts today; cleanse us from every sin and set us free. Guide and bless these men and women who have been sent to direct us to the center of Your will. I ask it in the name of Your Son, the living Savior, Jesus Christ. Amen."[2]

Endnotes

1. Psalm 64:4.

2. Reprinted by permission. This prayer is now being called "America's Prayer of Repentance."

Chapter 8

Pick Up This Torch . . . We Dare You!

"I want to feel you in my heart, mind, soul and life.
I want heads to turn in the halls when I walk by.
I want them to stare at me, watching and wanting
the light you've put in me.
I want you to overflow my cup with your Spirit.
I want so much from you.
I want you to use me to reach the unreached."

Personal Journal Entry, Rachel Joy Scott, March 1, 1998

I stood up to speak. Before me sat nearly 1,000 youths and youth leaders from 28 states and several foreign nations. Eager young faces met my gaze, their eyes sparkling with the anticipation that they were about to embark on a grand adventure. "They've reported for duty, Lord," I remember praying under my breath. "Now, help us equip them for war!"

The Columbine Torchgrab Youth Rally began on August 6 with a powerful sense of the presence of God. As we entered into worship and praise, I couldn't help but think about the second half of my dream from January 20, when the fear drained out of the faces of the youths and was replaced by that steely-eyed look of fervent determination. I had the distinct feeling that I was standing before the "Commissioned Officers" of a great army for Christ—an army that would march across the planet with the glory and power of God. A shiver ran up my spine. The trumpet was about to blow.

> "They've reported for duty, Lord. Now, help us equip them for war!"

From the first day of the Columbine disaster, I asked God how we might respond in a positive and proactive way in order to make sure that these young students had not died in vain. This young generation has been so wounded, so battered, so abused. Ron Luce, of the ministry Teen Mania, said it well: "We've produced a generation of broken hearts."[1] My heart yearns to help this youthful army rise up, equipped and trained, to give the devil some "payback."

At Rachel's funeral I was honored to issue a challenge to quite possibly the largest audience in the history of the planet to "pick up the torch" that Rachel and the other believing kids at Columbine had carried in their school. I received so many responses from those across the world who had taken that challenge to heart that my mind reeled. The constant theme of many of the responses was, "How can we respond and carry the torch in *our* city, (or school, or state)?"

Spontaneously, scores of rallies began to spring up across the nation. I spoke at several of them—at times alone, and at other times with Rachel's mom and stepfather, along with her sisters Bethanee and Dana. One of these, held in San Jose and organized by Pastor Dick Burnal and dozens of churches in the San Francisco Bay area, had an attendance of more than 16,000 people! Rachel's mother, Beth, thrilled that assembly with her words: "The devil thought he could get my daughter Rachel cheap, but that price is going up every day!" Bethanee and Dana shared with that huge assembly while under an unusually powerful anointing. A portion of Rachel's funeral, with my challenge to take up the torch Rachel carried, was presented. Thousands of youths leapt to their feet, held up their arms, and cheered. The powers of darkness were no doubt shaken that night!

The messages shared during the Columbine Torchgrab Youth Rally in Littleton will go down in history as pivotal to the next wave of God's moving in our world. Bob Weiner of Rock America Torch Rallies was highly instrumental in helping to bring together the finances, prayer support, advertising, and experienced know-how to make this one of the most successful rallies ever! Bob's challenge to the youth to go out into their schools and win ten persons and disciple them to do the same, was powerful! He laid a challenge out to those present to win a million new people to Christ by April 20, 2000.

We had some of the most effective and powerful youth leaders in America come and share at the rally. Eastman Curtis, Ron Luce, Cindy Jacobs, Kent Henry, Jeff Perry, Melody Green, and Bob Weiner imparted all they could to encourage and equip. Several youth from Columbine, who shared their experiences, raised the level of excitement and commitment to new heights. The local youth band, Tainted Vision, played a set of songs written especially for Columbine. Ron Luce spoke twice, sharing a riveting message of commitment. Last April, shortly after the Columbine bloodshed, Ron gathered 73,000 Christian teens from across America into the Silverdome in Detroit for a giant "Acquire the Fire" event. This was a strategic event, considering what had happened just a few days previous in Littleton. We were honored to have these brethren come to Littleton.

My wife, Claudia, wrote the following report on the Columbine Torchgrab Rally:

"Zealous teens from 28 states and Canada, Mexico, and Switzerland invaded Littleton, Colorado, to rally for a spiritual revolution of aggressive compassion in response to the bloodshed of innocent Christian martyrs at Columbine High School.

"Just a few miles away from the massacre, loud cries for a mighty revival to flood the nation's schools filled the atmosphere. From crescendos of elated rejoicing in worship to heart-wrenching weeping over a lost generation...God's presence sovereignly recruited every person into action.

"A sea of praying hands surrounded the father, brother, and sister of Rachel Scott, a victim of the shootings, after they gave strong testimonies of Rachel's strong faith and God's grace and mercy in sustaining them through her death. Her journal echoes her dedication to Christ regardless of ridicule... 'If I have to sacrifice everything for Jesus, I will.'

"Columbine student Valeen Schnurr gave her very first public testimony of how she survived after being shot over 12 times. She said 'Yes' in the library when asked by the gunmen if she believed in God.

"Action-provoking teachings and exhortations from Ron Luce, Eastman Curtis, Bruce Porter, Bob Weiner, Jeff Perry, Cindy Jacobs, and Melody Green gave rock-solid equipping for transforming the nation's youth and schools.

"Celebration Arts dancers, a teen group of dramatic dancers, performed a dance and poignant drama to the music of Delirious, telling the story of the torch being passed from Jesus to the early martyrs all the way to the Columbine martyrs and then to the audience. Stephanie Weiner choreographed and danced powerfully to 'I Surrender All.'

"A local youth band, Tainted Vision, who spent many cold nights after the tragedy singing and playing at the Clement Memorial Park in the rain and snow to comfort those mourning, performed an original song, 'I Never Really Learned How to Cry,' written about the Columbine tragedy.

"Kent Henry, a pioneer in the worship-psalmist ministry for decades, led the crowd in high praise and worship and stirred up new music ministries in the audience.

"The final evening closed with the challenge to take up the blood-stained torch of these young martyrs. Luminescent torches lit up the darkened auditorium symbolizing the pledge of many hundreds to be the light of Christ and living martyrs to their generation. Each delegate left armed with a 'TorchPack' bag filled with hundreds of dollars worth of evangelistic and equipping books, tapes, CDs, videos, and T-shirts donated by ministries around the country. They left to return to their mission stations in a blaze of glory."

*   *   *   *   *

Good Reports

"Wow is all I can say, and that word does not capture all that I gained from the rally! I took six kids from my youth group and they are totally on fire to evangelize kids at their schools and well trained to do it! One of the girls has already organized prayer groups to pray at each of the high schools in our district."

"The two young men that came from Baltimore were completely changed and matured into harvesters after the Torchgrab 1½ day boot camp! A passion was birthed for their destinies as Torch Bearers for the Gospel."

"Report after report of students starting prayer groups on campuses across the nation are flowing in. Prayer walking schools is commonplace. The fire is on!"

*   *   *   *   *

The front page of the Sunday *The Denver Post* the next morning featured a huge top, center page picture of the rally in full color that depicted a time of fervent prayer by several hundred participants for Rachel Scott's family. The press we received was incredibly positive and favorable. Since the rally, we've heard so many wonderful reports from around the country. God is surely moving!

Since April, I've continued to travel across the country sounding the trumpet call and encouraging youth and parents to take up the torch of the Littleton martyrs. We established a nonprofit organization called "Torchgrab Youth Ministries," of which Rachel's mom, Beth, is a member of the Board of Directors. We are hoping to interface with other organizations to reach this generation with the grace of God. The response has been very encouraging, as the stories and the challenge move people's hearts. If we are to see the great harvest we have all prayed for, it will surely come forth from these wonderful young people.[2]

According to *Business Week*, there are approximately 60 million kids in this upcoming generation of post-Gen-Xers who were born between 1979 and 1994.[3] Right now in the United States there are an estimated 25 million teens, and that number is anticipated to swell to more than 35 million in another seven or eight years. That represents a potentially huge army!

The world, and especially the devil, is not kicking back when it comes to reaching this huge block of young people! Huge companies that sell everything from chips to jeans are spending billions of dollars in advertising to capture their money! *Business Week* even reported recently on a youth-oriented company that boasted, "We are going to own this generation."[4] Time Warner, through their MTV subsidiary, has already said that they "own" this generation.

I have news for Madison Avenue, MTV, Hollywood, and all the other wannabe owners of the hearts and minds of this generation. *It's the top of the second inning with no outs, the bases are loaded with millions of youth who are hungry for God, and the Lord is just stepping up to the plate with no intention of bunting!*

E-mail Update
Thursday, May 20, 1999

A few items of news…

The makeshift memorials around Columbine have been removed. As I visited the area around Clement Park today, it was hard to find evidence that anything had ever happened there other than some obviously damaged turf on the lawns. The 13 crosses have been removed in order to satisfy the tiny secular minority who are so deeply offended at such obvious displays of Christian devotion. So many tears had been shed there, so many expressions of sorrow and grief. Could this actually be the place where thousands had come to stand in the rain and snow and mourn such loss?

The family of Rachel Scott has been greatly encouraged with news that Rachel answered bravely of her faith in God moments before the gunman held his weapon to her head and said, "Then go and be with Him now!"

The past few weeks have been especially difficult for the families of those who were slain. Mother's Day was particularly hard for all the moms. Rachel's mother has been so strong, and yet, one can easily see the strain on her soul. She has walked in such a graceful way through her pain and sorrow. Your prayers for her and all the other families have had a marvelous effect in lifting the burden of grieving for their slain children.

As some of you are now aware, one month after the slaughter at Columbine H.S., another student attacked his fellow students in Conyers, Georgia. Thankfully, no one was killed, but this event underscores what I've shared repeatedly. Columbine was a dress rehearsal of things to come…

Our nation is in a major moral crisis, and we now have a significant number of people, many of them quite young, who are prone to the

89

most vicious outbursts of violence. The politicians, political pundits, and talking heads of the media are wringing their hands and lamenting the presence of firearms, seeking some sort of "quick fix" to a much more profound problem.

They still don't get it.

Our present crisis of violence among our youth is, at the core, a SPIRITUAL problem. Unless we address the issue of the spiritual vacuum that exists in our nation's schools, all the laws, regulations, restrictions, metal detectors, armed guards, surveillance cameras, or whatever, will do exactly NOTHING to heal the situation! Determined evil will always find ways to circumvent any obstacle in its path.

I watched with great interest the televised visit of the President and First Lady with the students of Columbine today here in Denver. As the Superintendent of the Jefferson County Schools rose to speak, I noted that she acknowledged with swelling expressions of gratitude, the school officials, the psychologists, the police, fire and rescue personnel, the SWAT team, the FBI, the politicians, and the teachers. These all certainly deserved some recognition.

However, I couldn't help but notice that there was no place given for an invocation by a representative member of the local churches, which would have been most appropriate and appreciated. Also glaringly absent in her stirring accolades was any mention of God, or the scores of ministers, youth workers, Christian counselors, and countless church members from many congregations in the community who labored tirelessly (and continue to do so) to help the distressed families who had wounded or slain children. Please understand, those who truly serve the Lord would never seek praise or recognition. On the contrary, those who serve Christ do so most happily when in secret, for we know whom we serve and are assured of His approval and eternal reward.

I mention it only because the lack of acknowledgment of any meaningful contribution by the Christian community by the Superintendent or the President serves to illustrate the fact that in America today, we have a "religious apartheid" in operation. What sort of message does this lack of public recognition of Christian leadership in our community convey to our young people? Simply this, that Christian leadership, and indeed the Church itself, is irrelevant in any public forum or "important" discourse. Sadly, many of the kids have been "getting" the message loud and clear.

It is my firm belief that God is sovereignly moving by His mighty Spirit upon this generation of young people. I believe that we are about to witness the greatest ingathering of people to Christ ever witnessed since the Church was brought forth upon the earth. The true heroes will be the young people, anointed by God, who will overcome fear and intimidation and become bold beyond human explanation. They will not be religious in the normal sense of the word, but will be intensely sincere and completely intolerant of compromise with darkness. They will rebel against hypocrisy and traditions of men, overturning the tables of modern-day money changers who have defiled the Church with their love of and preoccupation with material comforts. They will be bold in the face of corrupt politicians, and some of them will spill their blood for the cause of Christ.

Some of these young activists will be hated by those who prefer their Christianity to be "lukewarm" and despised by those who have compromised the message of the gospel by accommodating the world's siren call to materialism. God will do this, for it is His anointing that will empower and give wisdom and inspired utterance to youthful lips that will confound the learned.

I believe we must do all we can to encourage and equip this band of young believers. One method of doing this is to hold several "Torch-Grab" rallies around the nation where we hope to impart some skills and spiritual tools that will aid our youth in their mission to reach this generation. We must either help them or get out of their way! They will not be stopped, for God has called them! The transmission of vision and destiny is the greatest heritage we may ever hope to impart to our young people!

Let us train and equip them to take back their schools! Let's give them the tools to be modern "Joans of Arc" who will lead their generation to great victories!

Sincerely in God's love,
Pastor Bruce

Endnotes

1. Ron Luce, "The Cry of a Lost Generation," *Charisma Magazine* (September 1999): 49.

2. See pages 129-131 for a list of recommended youth ministries.

3. Ellen Newborne and Kathleen Kerwin, "Generation Y," *Business Week* (February 15, 1999).

4. Ellen Newborne, "We Are Going to Own This Generation," *Business Week* (February 15, 1999).

Chapter 9

The Last Full Measure
of Devotion

"You want to know what I feel?
What I think about constantly?
What is on my heart?
God.
Seriously, He is all I think about.
I want to serve Him so much.
I'm sorry if I come on so strong.
I just wish you knew how it feels.
I just feel so happy and fulfilled."
Personal Journal Entry, Rachel Joy Scott, March 9, 1998

Standing before long rows of white crosses at Fort Logan National Cemetery last Memorial Day, I watched as a group of young Civil Air Patrol Cadets planted small United States flags before each of the graves of the veterans buried there, then stepped back and smartly saluted before moving on to the next gravestone. My heart swelled with pride as these youths, the finest young men and women in our nation, bestowed honor upon those who served their country.

As a personal outreach project, I serve as an officer with the Civil Air Patrol, the official auxiliary of the USAF. My duties include teaching Moral Leadership, in which I seek to influence young men and women in the Cadet program to pursue and live the highest standards of ethics and good character. It's a labor of love, and the 60 to 80 cadets I work with in our squadron come from a wide variety of backgrounds and religious convictions. The one thing that is common to them all, however, is their desire to pursue a higher standard.

Each year on Memorial Day weekend I lead these young men and women to the National Veteran's Cemetery at Fort Logan to place flags on the graves there. It may seem a trivial thing to some, but there is something amazingly powerful about showing honor to whom honor is due. When I was a younger and more foolish man, I did not always appreciate the sacrifices made by the men and women who defended our freedom. Then, as a Vietnam veteran myself, I returned home bitter and disillusioned after serving for a year and a half. Being disdained by those I sought to serve was a

> "That we here highly resolve that these dead shall not have died in vain...."

painful experience when I came home. In my more mature years I've come to believe that, without honor, we cannot long endure as a nation. It is a solemn duty for each of us to highly esteem those who have served us through their sacrifices.

When walking among the resting places of those who served their nation with honor, one can sense a powerful heritage and continuity, a link with the past. When I'm in that place, I cannot help but think of the words of Army General Douglas MacArthur, who said in his farewell address to the U.S. Military Academy at West Point on May 12, 1962:

> "The long gray line has never failed us. Were you to do so, a million ghosts in olive drab, in brown khaki, in blue and gray would rise from their white crosses, thundering those magic words: duty, honor, country!"

As President Abraham Lincoln once stated so eloquently in his famous Gettysburg Address:

> "It is rather for us to be here dedicated to the great task remaining before us...that from these honored dead we take increased devotion to that cause for which they gave the last full measure of devotion...that we here highly resolve that these dead shall not have died in vain..."

The statement, "that we here highly resolve that these dead shall not have died in vain," echoes in my heart and mind. Shall these have died in vain? I say never! The compelling, high calling of God in Christ will never allow that! I believe that we stand at the threshold of a great awakening, a massive move of God's Spirit that will sweep aside the cobwebs of dead religion and replace it with the fresh breezes of God's manifest presence in our midst. Every lofty thought, every clanging cymbal of human vanity, and every arrogant expression of man's puny intellect will crumble before the power of God's predetermined counsel. Conscience forces me to do all I personally can, to make certain that these young people who died at Columbine "shall not have died in vain."

*   *   *   *   *

I visited another grave that morning. A few miles away lies another very special veteran, a casualty from a different war: 17-year-old Rachel Joy Scott. Even though I was still in uniform, I felt it was most appropriate to visit Rachel's resting place, for she, like so many who died with her, are truly veterans of war. Unlike the last time I was at that spot during her funeral, with the freshly fallen snow and the mournful presence of so many in grief, this time the air was warm and carried the smell of fresh spring flowers in bloom. It was a quiet spring morning, with bright sunshine and the chirping of birds.

I was touched by the addition of the 13 wooden crosses that had been placed there just before the Memorial Day weekend. These crosses, rejected by the City of Littleton Park authorities, now find a permanent resting place here also, among the dead. I was moved at the sight of these symbols of such devotion and love, yet deeply disturbed by the fact that in spite of the horrific deaths of so many innocent Christian children, they could not be welcomed in a public place among the living. I cannot help but wonder what goes on in the hearts of those who disdain and reject the symbols that were most meaningful in life to those slain.

Thirteen crosses have been placed as a memorial, but only two of the Columbine victims are actually buried at this site. As I approached Rachel's grave, I noticed that Corey DePooter, another slain student, now rested beside her. The magnitude of the loss of the 12 students and one teacher, Mr. Sanders, broke afresh upon my heart and mind, and I struggled to remain composed. Walking past each of the 13 crosses, I paused to look once again at the pictures of the slain posted upon each one. It's almost more than the mind can take in. If people should die in a tornado, in an automobile accident, from a disease, or in another unavoidable tragedy, we can somehow more easily accept it. However, when such wanton, deliberate killing takes place, we are all disturbed in a much deeper way.

Withdrawing out of the warm sunlight there in that cemetery, I sat down in the shadow of a large statue of Christ situated near Rachel's grave. The statue has such a look of compassion on the face, and the arms are raised in a gesture of mournful acceptance toward the graves of Rachel and Corey. In the solitude of that special place, I could almost hear the voice of Jesus weeping and asking, "Behold, what have you done to My precious little ones?" I sat under the shadow of the Almighty and wept bitter tears. Tears for Rachel. Tears for Cassie, Kyle, Steven, Lauren, Kelly, and for Mr. Sanders. Tears for Isaiah, Dan, John, Matt, Corey, and Daniel. And yes, even tears for Eric and Dylan, who were lost children growing up in a broken world that sometimes fosters unspeakable evil in those who allow themselves to be enticed by it.

*   *   *   *   *

Our community was shocked yet again by the tragic suicide of Carla Hochhalter, mother of Columbine survivor, Anne Marie. Ms. Hochhalter represents, in my mind, Eric and Dylan's fourteenth victim. Anne Marie barely survived multiple gunshot wounds in the attack, and she must now face not only a future of partial paralysis, but also a life devoid of a mother. The pain and trauma the victim families continue to endure is beyond description.

Kelly Ann Fleming, one of the Columbine victims, was a deeply contemplative person. Like Rachel, Kelly seemed also to have had a darker premonition of her times. Her mother shared with me the following poem she found among Kelly's writings:

Can That Be?
I step outside what did I hear?
I heard the whispers and
The cries of people's fear,
The loneliness of wisdom,
Can that be?
The sad, sad, sorrow that I see,
That is past in the tree.

Is it true? Can it be real?
Can I let them know how I really feel?
The things that I have seen,
The things that I have felt,
The feelings of sorrow that
I hope will soon melt.
I walked through the distances
And thought how it should be,
Of the smiles and the laughter,
That is what I thought it should be.
But can that be?
I walked past the dark houses,
And crossed the open fields.
I walked to the tree to kneel.
I took a deep long breath,
Then I closed my eyes.
I counted to three,
Then I opened my eyes,
I was in my room,
That was a surprise.
But then I had seen that it was just a dream.
I walked to the window and pulled on the string.
What a surprise to see the sunrise.
In the distance were children with laughter and happiness,
That was the thought that I like to see!
But of course can that really be?
Or can this be another dream?

Kelly Ann Fleming

Kelly's mother, Dee Fleming, is one of the brokenhearted Littleton mothers who lost her precious child in the Columbine massacre. Several weeks after Kelly died, Dee penned the following words to her little girl. Dee eloquently captured with these words the collective sense of grief and sorrow that all the other victim families experienced.

98

My dearest Kelly,

Once again I walk into my room and past your picture. Those sparkling blue eyes gaze back at me. Your long brown hair so thick and shining. I see that sweet little hint of a smile. This time, however, like so many other times, I am once again thrown into a complete panic. My heart begins to race with such speed, I begin at once to feel as though it will explode from my chest. I can feel the blood literally drain from my very being. My arms and legs begin to tingle and I am overcome with the knowledge that I will never ever see you again. My sweet Kelly is no longer here. How could this happen? Can you actually be gone? This just can't be really happening, I tell myself; and yet I know it to be true.

You did nothing wrong. Just went to school and into the library to write a story or a letter before meeting your friends for second lunch. Then, within minutes, all hell broke loose around you. Huddled alone under a table listening as the bombs were exploding. Listening...to screams of terror all around. Listening...as the others were being taunted, shot and murdered. Listening...as they were coming ever closer to where you hid. Scared to death of what was going on around you. Wondering what should you do, with nowhere to go. And then, it was your turn. What did they say to you? Did they look into your beautiful blue eyes so filled with tears and terror? Did they laugh? And then you were gone in an instant. Blown away by some soulless, inhumane being. Killed by pure evil and then left to lie there for oh so long.

I am so sorry, Kelly, so very, very sorry. All your life I tried to keep you safe. I was always there to shelter you and protect you. And that day you went to school, and I didn't think I had to worry because kids should be safe in their schools. I was wrong, and I'm sorry. I know we let you and the others down.

The nation and the world mourn your death. There were so many who wanted to ease our pain and help in any way possible. Thousands have sent us their condolences and prayers. You were so lovingly remembered by many who knew you and by many others who never had the opportunity and never will. You are a priceless gift of God and can never be replaced. I want to make sure the world never forgets you and the others.

My heart slowly returns to normal as I manage to catch my breath. The sheer terror of another realization that I no longer have my beautiful baby girl with me subsides. I lovingly kiss the top of your head as I pass by your picture, just as I did so many times when you would be standing here beside me.

I love you, Kelly, and I miss you,
Mom

*   *   *   *   *

Well-intentioned counselors seek to help us "get over it and move on with our lives." Occasionally I hear people say things like, "I'm tired of hearing about Columbine. Why can't we just move on?" Personally, I don't want to ever "get over" this! I want the memory of Columbine to *howl* in my mind and heart as a constant reminder of how broken this present world is and how desperately people need a revelation of the love and grace of Christ!

I've learned to hate "normal." It lulls one to sleep with its promise of comfort and false security. Just when you begin to relax, just when you allow yourself the luxury of thinking that maybe, just maybe, this present world isn't so bad after all, you are rudely awakened to the harsh reality of sin in all its hideous myriad forms.

Jesus was a "man of sorrows and acquainted with grief."[1] Oh, He certainly had a good laugh sometimes, and I have the definite impression from the Scriptures that He was even a bit mischievous on occasion with His disciples. Underneath it all, though, He carried

100

Courtesy of Bruce Porter

"I want to stay in a state of continual brokenhearted devotion to the high calling of God, realizing that His good news is the world's *only* hope! If this attitude defines a dysfunctional way of life, then I shall embrace it as a friend and gift."—Bruce Porter within Himself an understanding that people at their very best are lost children, often given to the most cruel expressions of selfishness. He had an abiding sense of mission, for He knew that as the slain Lamb of God, He was our *only* hope for gaining freedom from our slavery to sin and rescuing a brokenhearted world. Jesus Christ is an example to us of giving the full measure of devotion...and as we respond to Him, our nation will experience the healing and peace of God.

Endnote

1. Isaiah 53:3 NKJV.

Chapter 10

Where Was God When Columbine Happened?

"The problem of reconciling human suffering
with the existence of a God who loves,
is only insoluble so long as we attach
a trivial meaning to the word 'love.' "
C.S. Lewis

Since the tragedy at Columbine High School, and now since the more recent killing of the innocents at Wedgwood Baptist Church in Fort Worth, Texas, people have frequently asked me, "Where was God when these tragedies happened?" To be honest, I've tried to dodge this age-old, controversial question, raised with complete predictability each and every time something horrible happens in this present world. I've finally decided to "weigh in" on this issue here in the back of the book. Some of what I share here may be troubling, especially if you think that God's interactions with the world depends upon you. I'm willing to take the heat by tackling this question, and I recognize and respect the fact that many sincere, godly people will differ with some of my assertions. Nevertheless, I hope that what I share here will promote a dialogue and drive people to their knees and Bibles to satisfy themselves about the truth or falsehood of what I say.

The question, "Where was God when this happened?" reveals a few basic assumptions about the nature and character of God in many people's minds. The logic often used is this: "If God is truly good, merciful, and just, then how could He allow evil to happen to 'good' people?" Theologians have wrestled with this fundamental question for thousands of years; however, there are some points that I think we need to consider as we look back at history, especially biblical history. The inescapable fact is that, down through the centuries, much evil has befallen righteous men and women while they faithfully served God. Many of these individuals were clearly in the perfect will of God, and yet they suffered many trials and tribulations at the hands of wicked men.

There are some who would sincerely say that people who suffer or die in the service of Christ are somehow flawed in their grasp of scriptural principles relating to "victory" in this present world. If this is the case, then we must conclude that virtually every early Church believer, including the apostles, failed to appropriate the full promises of God and walk in "victorious faith."

All the early apostles suffered for Christ. They were called upon to give testimony of their faith in Jesus with their own blood. According to tradition, the following were their fates:

- Matthew suffered martyrdom by being slain with a sword at a distant city of Ethiopia.

- Mark died at Alexandria after being brutally dragged through the streets of the city.

- Luke was hanged upon an olive tree in Greece.

- John was put in a caldron of boiling oil, but he miraculously escaped death and was afterward banished to the island of Patmos to starve.

- Peter was crucified at Rome with his head downward.

- James the Greater was beheaded at Jerusalem.

- James the Less was thrown from a high pinnacle of the temple and then beaten to death with a fuller's club.

- Bartholomew was flayed alive.

- Andrew was bound to a cross, from which he preached to his persecutors until he died.

- Thomas was run through the body with a lance at Coromandel in the East Indies.

- Jude was shot to death with arrows.

- Matthias was first stoned and then beheaded.

- Barnabas of the Gentiles was stoned to death at Salonica.

- Paul, after various tortures and persecutions, was finally beheaded at Rome by the Emperor Nero.

Where was God when these beloved, faithful servants were suffering and dying for their testimony? I would answer that God was right where He was when His own Son was crucified for our sin. The Father suffered with Him and them—and He was touched with their pain and mourned their deaths.

Precious in the sight of the Lord is the death of His saints (Psalm 116:15 NKJV).

The word for "precious" in this verse is the Hebrew word *yaqar*, which can be translated "valuable, brightness, costly, excellent, precious."[1]

I believe that God grieves over the death of His children more profoundly than we are humanly able to comprehend. If this is so, one might ask, "Then why doesn't He stop it?" From our human perspective it seems reasonable to question God. If He truly is loving, merciful, and compassionate, then why would He allow bad things to happen to "good" people, and especially to innocent children?

The main reason we struggle with this question is that we have a very limited perspective on reality. I have an image in my mind from a recent cartoon film where some ants are going about their business when, suddenly, a lawnmower passes overhead. They cannot begin to comprehend what that big, noisy, windy, whirling thing is. They have no frame of reference for what they're seeing, and they can only vaguely describe what their senses are telling them about this huge phenomenon.

When we try to comprehend the ways of God with our limited capacity as fallen human beings, we are very much like those ants. All we can do is scurry about and try to stay out of the way of the "big, noisy, windy, whirling thing." Some struggle with this idea, for we prefer to think of ourselves in a much more favorable light intellectually. We like to think that we have things pretty well figured out, and it's frightening for us to be faced with a Being so immensely transcendent to us as to stagger our imagination.

Oh, what a wonderful God we have! How great are His riches and wisdom and knowledge! How impossible it is for us to understand His decisions and His methods! For who can know what the Lord is thinking? Who knows enough to be His counselor? And who could ever give Him so much that He would have to pay it back? For everything comes from Him; everything

106

exists by His power and is intended for His glory. To Him be glory evermore. Amen (Romans 11:33-36).

For as the heavens are higher than the earth, so are My ways higher than your ways, and My thoughts than your thoughts (Isaiah 55:9 NKJV).

One of my personal hobbies is amateur astronomy. From my studies of the stellar heavens, I can say with some confidence that the heavens are indeed quite a bit higher than the earth. In fact, the very nearest star we observe is Alpha Centauri C (Proxima), which is about 4.2 light-years away! That means it takes more than four years for light to reach us from that star, traveling at approximately 186,000 miles per second! The Milky Way, our home galaxy, of which our solar system is a part, is about 100,000 light-years across and contains several hundreds of billions of stars of various sizes and colors like our sun.

Beyond our home galaxy, our nearest galactic neighbor is M-31, or the Great Andromeda Galaxy. It's the most distant object we can see with the naked eye, about 2 million light-years distant. Beyond this are many hundreds of billions of huge galaxies, each containing hundreds of billions of stars. Then there are billions more of huge clusters of galaxies, and beyond them are clusters of clusters of galaxies that form gigantic walls of galaxies...whew! Based upon Isaiah 55:9, I think the Lord is trying to tell us that, compared to Him, we're somewhat cerebrally challenged (to put it politely).

When we try to comprehend the workings and purposes of God, we invariably make the mistake of putting Him in boxes that make Him more manageable in our own understanding. This is unavoidable. Why? He created us in His image and likeness, and we yearn, hunger, and thirst to know Him! However, we must remain humble and recognize that we are dealing with a Being so amazing, so powerful, so intelligent, so knowledgeable, and so wonderful, that it will take all eternity to discover Him!

Sometimes God is gracious and reveals the "why" of what He is doing. This is especially important to us when tragedies happen and our hearts are broken by the sorrows of this present sin-sick, broken world. We are so quick to toss out easy answers as to why things happen. We glibly consign every seemingly "bad" thing that happens to the devil. When things go well in our estimation, then we say, "That's God!" In all of it, we are called upon to trust God, and this is the greatest test of faith we shall endure in this world.

Part of our limited perspective is due to our concept of time. We in this world experience time as a series of events occurring one after another. This is how we define past, present, and future. This also can be called "linear awareness." It is very much like feeling your way along a string. The point of the string you are holding at the moment is the "present." The part you just left is the "past," and the part you are moving on to is the "future." Now, consider for a moment the following concept: The past, present, and future actually exist as one simultaneous event from God's perspective. God experiences reality outside of time, and the past, present, and future are all one simultaneous experience for Him. In other words, all events at all times are His eternal experience.

Picture a ball. If you draw a line around the middle of it and place your finger on a specific point somewhere along that line, you are demonstrating our human experience of time. You can only exist at one point along the line, or one place at a time. You're not omnipresent, but God is! Now, place your finger on the top of the ball. From this spot you can contact every point along the line around the ball at the same time! This is God's experience! He sees the end from the beginning. He lives and dwells at all times, in all places, and knows all things. Not a single atom in the entire universe is outside His complete awareness of its status, position, and function.

Can you fathom the mysteries of God? Can you probe the limits of the Almighty? They are higher than the heavens—what can you do? They are deeper than the depths of the grave—what can you know? Their measure is longer than the earth and wider than the sea (Job 11:7-9 NIV).

Why do bad things happen to good people? The truth is, we simply don't know from our present limited perspective. It's clear from the Scriptures that God has the final word on everything that happens. He is the Alpha and the Omega, the Beginning and the End, the First and the Last. And yet, we are troubled about the inequity and injustice we clearly witness in the world. Could it be that everything that happens—even the things that are clearly the work of the devil himself—happens within the larger purpose and plan of God to bring about a greater glory? Can we actually believe that, ultimately, everything is going according to God's predetermined counsels and purposes? Consider Jesus. When He stood before Pilate, He refused to speak.

"Do you refuse to speak to me?" Pilate said. "Don't You realize I have power either to free You or to crucify You?" Jesus answered, "You would have no power over Me if it were not given to you from above..." (John 19:10-11 NIV).

Consider the importance of this! Jesus clearly understood something we scarcely dare to think about! Pilate was acting under the authority and carrying out the will of God Himself when he had Jesus beaten nearly to death, mocked, spat upon, and eventually crucified! Look at this Scripture:

He who did not spare His own Son, but delivered Him up for us all, how shall He not with Him also freely give us all things? (Romans 8:32 NKJV)

Who delivered Jesus up for crucifixion? Was it Pilate? The Romans? The Jews? None of them did, though they all unwittingly played out their roles in the larger plan of God.

God Almighty has a larger range of purpose, wisdom, and understanding than we are humanly capable of understanding! If we lose sight of this fact, we will fall into the trap of what I would describe as "religious schizophrenia," a trap that many of our brethren have been snared into because of our faulty understanding of God. Schizophrenia is defined as "a psychosis characterized by withdrawal from reality and by highly variable behavioral and intellectual disturbances."[2] Sounds like some people I've met at church!

We often declare, "Jesus is Lord of all!" or, "God is in control!" However, when tribulation, suffering, persecution, or even tragedies like Columbine occur, we then fall back on, "Look what the devil did!" By God's grace may we come up to a higher level of revelation and see the larger picture. God is indeed in control, and He is indeed "Lord of all." But we can't have it both ways and be consistent.

So we return to the question, "Where was God when the massacre took place at Columbine High School?" For that matter, where was He during the countless other slaughters, genocides, ethnic cleansings, murders, persecutions, pogroms, and sundry holocausts that have plagued our world since the fall of Adam in the garden? Well, believe it or not, He is still right where He has always been, loving His people, and, from a perspective far beyond any human comprehension, governing the affairs of men as it pleases Him.

Someone may now ask, "Are you intimating that God murdered those children at Columbine?" This is the wrong question, which is based upon a flawed comprehension of the majesty of Him who is, who was, and is to come. He is not a cruel God or a killer of innocent children; rather He was aware that all these things were going to happen, and He was prepared with a complete plan and purpose for a greater outcome! I refer you again to the quote at the beginning of this chapter:

> *"The problem of reconciling human suffering*
> *with the existence of a God who loves,*
> *is only insoluble so long as we attach*
> *a trivial meaning to the word 'love.' "*
> C.S. Lewis

On the weekend before the Columbine massacre, Larry Pambianco, a youth pastor, was conducting a youth gathering in Denver. A substantial group of young people was in attendance that night when Larry was suddenly overtaken with an impression from the Lord and spoke out. "Someone here is planning to kill some people," he said. No one responded. At that moment, Larry had no way of knowing that out in that crowd stood the solitary, brooding figure of a young man named Eric Harris. Did God know the end from the beginning? Did He foresee what was about to happen the following Tuesday? I think He did. Why didn't He stop it? I don't know, and neither does anyone else other than God Himself.

Was God orchestrating this drama? Are we all playing out roles in a master script? To some, it would seem so. Does God have a plan He's working out to show His glory to the entire earth? We know from Scripture that He certainly is. How are we to react to this?

My personal take on all this is simply this: *trust.*

God is asking us to *trust* Him! This is hard for self-willed, self-determined persons to accept. Our entire culture is based upon the assumption of personal ambition and that "God helps those who help themselves." We are all conditioned to react to the world as if everything is entirely up to us, and if anything good is to happen, then we must determine it. If anything bad is to be prevented, then we must depend upon ourselves to do something about it! For the "hopeful humanist" the credo is, "No God will save us; we must save ourselves!"

This kind of thinking has permeated the Christian Church to such an extent that whole movements and denominational sects have been created to further the belief that "everything is up to us"! Oh, to be sure, we give lip service to the precept of prayer, and we mouth without comprehension the words of Scriptures where even Jesus Himself said, "...Your will be done on earth as it is in heaven."[3] We all seem to have a pretty clear idea in our own minds what God's will is in every situation, and we instinctively resist any suggestion that God might also work in ways that seem contrary to what we prefer to believe.

Columbine was a spiritual event, known of God before it happened. The overwhelming evidence we have from Rachel's writings is that she was being prepared for what was about to happen. I'm also certain that each and every other child who lost his or her life that day was not forgotten by our heavenly Father. He knew and loved each and every one, and His mercy and compassion toward them was no less. We can battle it, argue against it, get angry, throw dirt in the air, or do whatever we like, but one way or another God will accomplish His purposes on earth—in spite of what we think about it. *He* is Lord, and He thinks on an infinitely higher level than we do. We have His promise in Romans 8:28: "And we know that all things work together for good to those who love God, to those who are the called according to His purpose."[4]

> *Then I heard a loud voice saying in heaven, "Now salvation, and strength, and the kingdom of our God, and the power of His Christ have come, for the accuser of our brethren, who accused them before our God day and night, has been cast down. And they overcame him by the blood of the Lamb and by the word of their testimony, and they did not love their lives to the death"* (Revelation 12:10-11 NKJV).

So it is with the life and death of Rachel and the other people at Columbine. Their legacy will live on as multitudes of young people draw strength and courage from their faithful testimony. And the martyrs' torch will continue to be lifted high, penetrating and challenging the darkness, revealing to the world the light and long of Jesus Christ through servants who love Him more than their own lives.

Endnotes

1. James Strong, *Strong's Exhaustive Concordance of the Bible* (Peabody, Massachusetts: Hendrickson Publishers, n.d.), *yagar* (#H3368).

2. *American Heritage Dictionary* CD-ROM, Word Star Intl., 1991, HMCo, 1991.

3. Luke 11:2 NKJV.

4. NKJV.

Chapter 11

Rachel's Challenge

I am absolutely certain that if Rachel Scott could signal something to us now, if she could deliver a challenge to the world, the essence of it would be found in the message she left us in the following poem.

What if you were to die today?
What would happen to you?
Where would you go?

Tomorrow is not a promise, but a chance,
It may not be there for you.

After death, then what?
Where will you spend your eternity?

Will you have an eternal life without our loving father,
or will you be ripped from the arms of your savior Jesus Christ?

ETERNITY IS IN YOUR HANDS...CHANGE IT!

Rachel Joy Scott

I know that you have been touched by the presence and grace of God while reading this book. My prayer is that the examples of Rachel and the other precious souls who lost their lives at Columbine will embolden you to sincerely take up the torch they carried and dedicate the remaining beats of your heart to His purposes. Will you be a martyr?

The term *martyr* comes from the Greek word *martus*, which simply means "a witness."[1] It does not necessarily mean, as is often assumed, "a person who dies for what he believes." It certainly can be used in that way, but not exclusively.

Followers of Jesus Christ are called to be "living witnesses" or "living martyrs." It is unlikely that we will have to face death for our Christian faith. Each of us, however, should live our lives in such a way that we have already settled the issue of our death before it actually happens. When we give our lives to Jesus, they are not ours any longer. We are dead to our own will and desires, and alive to His plans and purposes for us.

> He is honored and glorified when we are "living martyrs" serving Him and not ourselves.

God is certainly glorified when someone dies for his faith in Him. But He is also glorified when we *live* for Him! He is honored and glorified when we are "living martyrs" serving Him and not ourselves. As wonderful as Heaven will be, we must be about our Father's work here on earth—loving people, helping people, and sharing the good news of Jesus as long as breath is within us.

For the Christian who has gone beyond the unscriptural paradigm of "Jesus in *my life*" to "*Jesus* in my life," who has dared to see his relationship with God as an all-consuming relationship that influences every decision, the fear of death is no longer a controlling factor.

In a very positive sense, a believer in Christ who fears nothing but God, hates nothing but sin, and loves people as God loves them, is virtually unstoppable! To live without fear of what men may do is an awesome freedom! Without that freedom we are all too soon intimidated into silence by the threats of the bullies of this world!

Jesus wants us to primarily *live* for Him, not die for Him! Should we be chosen for such an honor as death for our faith, we can be sure that we will have all the grace needed to do exactly that! It is, without any question, an awesome honor to be called upon to sign our life's testimony in the world with the crimson stain of our own lifeblood. However, God needs His people active in this present world to reach out to those who have yet to see Light! He has no hands but our hands!

Someone sent me the following poem. I think it's apropos.

When I Say...
When I say..."I am a Christian"
I'm not shouting "I am saved!"
I'm whispering "I get lost!"
That is why I chose this way.

When I say..."I am a Christian"
I don't speak of this with pride.
I'm confessing that I stumble
and need someone to be my guide.

When I say..."I am a Christian"
I'm not trying to be strong.
I'm professing that I am weak
and pray for strength to carry on.

When I say..."I am a Christian"
I'm not bragging of success.
I'm admitting I have failed
and cannot ever pay the debt.

When I say..."I am a Christian"
I'm not claiming to be perfect,
my flaws are too visible
but God believes I'm worth it.

When I say..."I am a Christian"
I still feel the sting of pain
I have my share of heartaches
which is why I seek His name.

When I say..."I am a Christian"
I do not wish to judge.
I have no authority.
I only know I am loved.

Author Unknown

Rachel knew and understood this truth. She struggled, as every Christian does if he or she is secure enough to admit it, with temptation and discouragement. She struggled and overcame by the word of her testimony and by the blood of the Lamb, and she loved not her life unto death. Rachel's life in this world was brief. Our broken hearts and painful emotions cry out that it was far too brief. However, when we look with the eyes of eternity, we see a larger picture. Rachel was clearly prepared for what happened to her. She had her bags packed. She was ready. Are you?

The way to get ready is to make a decision...to make the choice to become a "living martyr" and give the rest of your life to Jesus Christ. It is a decision to turn away from doing things your own way (which is "sin") and choosing *His* way. Jesus died on the cross, then rose from the grave three days later, forever conquering the power of death. Jesus Christ willingly gave His life for you...are you willing to give your life to Him? Are you ready to invite Jesus into your heart as King and Lord of all? Do you want forgiveness for your sins?

If you've answered "yes" to those questions, then I invite you to have a simple conversation with God. It's commonly called a prayer, but it really is a conversation...

Heavenly Father, I believe that Jesus died on the cross for me and rose again. I have sinned against You by going my own way. I want forgiveness for all my sins. Father, I give You my life to do with as You wish. I want Jesus Christ to come into my life and into my heart as Lord and King. This I ask in Jesus' name. Amen.

If you prayed this sincerely, you can be assured upon the authority of God's Word that you are now a child of God.[2] You may feel emotional, or you may not. It makes no difference! You'll never be alone again. No matter what your circumstance, God has promised never to leave you or forsake you.[3] He's a friend who sticks closer than a brother![4] You can face anything that this crazy, broken world can dish out and draw from a limitless source of courage that flows from the presence of God.

Now, allow Him to be your strength, your hope, your source, and your desire. Spend time alone with Him. Get out under the stars at night and marvel at His awesome creation! Take time to experience the wonder of all He has made, and tell Him how much you appreciate it! As you grow spiritually, He'll startle you with His awesome presence in interesting and amazing ways. Get close with other believers who will encourage you and teach you new things about His love, grace, and mercy. Ask God to help you to find a church full of people who worship Jesus as Savior and Lord and who genuinely and sincerely love people.

*   *   *   *   *

After you have taken the first step and given your life to Christ, every day will hold new adventures. Every day also will present you with the same basic challenge: to live for Jesus and not for yourself.

This generation is the object of intense warfare. Listen to the sound of distant thunder and the trumpet blast of God's calling as it draws near. How will you respond? It is a call to heavenly arms, a call to spiritual battle. Will you step out of the overpopulated ranks of indifference, apathy, and fear and take your place in destiny as a spiritual warrior?

There is a torch waiting for your willing hand. This torch of Christian witness burns with white-hot coals taken from under the very altar of God's throne. This sacred flame has cast its light into the passages of human history for thousands of years, bringing light to mankind's darkness.

In some periods of history that flame was seen but dimly, and, in equal measure, human misery increased. However, in each and every epoch, when darkness threatened to extinguish that flickering flame of truth, when all hope seemed lost, there were those heroes of faith who boldly answered the battle cry of God's holy angels and rose up in the power and anointing of the Lord. As those heroes held high once again that eternal flame of the truth of Christ's gospel before the world, their torches blazed with the glory of 10,000 suns, shattering the darkness around them!

To be sure, many of those torchbearers paid dearly for their obedience to the heavenly call. The signature of their faithful testimony was often the crimson stain of their lifeblood lovingly poured out on the byways of human indifference and trampled underfoot by uncomprehending fools.

However, in each case there have been those who beheld the faithfulness of the bearers of God's holy flame who went before them, drew strength from their example, and, reaching down, once again raised up that bloodstained torch to blaze afresh in a new generation.

Rachel, Cassie, John, Valeen, and others who were killed or wounded on that fateful day at Columbine, carried torches. Some of their lights were noticed more than others, yet they all held a portion of the holy flame.

Scores of determined and courageous young people are reaching out and taking up the torch yet again, and the light of God's love and grace is growing brighter each day in the halls of our schools across the nation. Thousands upon thousands of souls, of young and old alike, are hearing the heavenly call, the call which I have put into printed form and now issue to *you*, the reader:

"Who will take up the martyrs' torch, which fell from these faithful hands?"

Rachel Joy Scott carried a torch—a torch of truth, a torch of compassion, a torch of love, a torch of the good news of Jesus Christ her Lord, whom she was not ashamed of, even in her hour of death. The torch has fallen from Rachel's hand. Will *you* pick it up again?

Pick up the torch that Rachel carried! Pick it up and hold it high. Stop being a victim. Rise above passivity and conformity. Be proactive! Speak to the culture you live in and declare a spiritual revolution of compassion, mercy, and love...and forsake violence.

I challenge you to stand up, right now, where you are, and say:

"I will live for Jesus Christ and not for myself! I will lift my voice in this generation and declare the truth and the righteous standards of the Kingdom of God! I will carry, with bold proclamation, the martyrs' torch!"

Endnotes

1. James Strong, *Strong's Exhaustive Concordance of the Bible* (Peabody, Massachusetts: Hendrickson Publishers, n.d.), ***martus*** (#G3144).

2. See John 1:12; Romans 10:13.

3. Hebrews 13:5.

4. See Proverbs 18:24.

Addendum

Here is a sampling of the hundreds of e-mail responses we received in the months following the Columbine massacre. I sense a new breeze blowing in the Church of America, and I am very encouraged by the boldness that Rachel and the other martyrs' courage has inspired.

Pastor Porter,

Hi. I was moved deeply by the testimony Rachel gave... When I heard about Rachel, I just started to cry. Her testimony has made me stronger. Now, I want to take up the torch.

C.H.

Dear Bruce and Claudia,

We were touched and moved by your singing and sermon at the service for Rachel Scott. I believe that you impacted everyone there, especially the youth. Our kids were very impacted by your sermon, so much so, that they made paper torches in the car afterwards, saying that they were taking up Rachel's torch. I saw a few of the youth as they were leaving the service lifting their arms in the air while walking to their cars.

M.S. & S.S.

Dear Pastor,

Thank you for taking the time to keep me updated. I am sharing your words with everyone here and forwarding them to those I know all over the world. You and all the families have been in our thoughts and prayers. We know that the Lord is using this situation to touch many lives. We know that what the devil has meant for evil God is going to use for good… My prayer, like yours, is that the Christian martyrs' torch of truth will be picked up all across this nation and world…

P.R.

Pastor,

I am from Holyoke, Massachusetts, and I just wanted to let you know that I will proudly take the torch that Rachel once held.

M.M.

Pastor Porter,

…We believe that the only hope for our families, our churches, our towns, our state, our country, and our world is the risen Savior! We would love to help "hold the torch," and want to organize a Christian crusade across the country so that those who lost their lives will not have died in vain. It's time to reclaim our communities!

M.M.

Pastor,

I am a middle school counselor in a public school in Ferndale, WA, a little community in the far corner of the Pacific NW. I read your e-mail, and I would like to do something to help our youth in my church and, hopefully, in our school to "pick up the torch." Thank you for your unexpected leadership role because of this horrible event.

M.C.

Dear Pastor,

I too am a viewer of the CNN coverage of the services performed in Littleton. With the call to carry the torch, both my girls raised their hand. I have never been more proud of my girls. I just felt compelled to let you know that we in Georgia share in your sorrow for what has happened to your community. We have shed tears just as you have for the fallen and for the Godlessness that has seemed rampant in our world today.

T.M.

Dearest Pastor Porter,

First, I want to express my deepest sympathy… I received the letter you wrote from a friend just this morning and wanted to respond. First of all thank you. It was a wonderful, touching letter and I was touched reading it. I, like millions others, sat in front of the television, clutching my three small children with tears streaming down my face. All I could say or think was "Dear Lord, Dear Lord." I also watched Rachel's funeral. It was awesome to see so many of the young people standing up, committing to carry Rachel's torch! Even in my living room in Birmingham, Alabama, I could feel the Holy Spirit there. It was…wow. I want to tell you that as I pray for the families, teachers, and officials, of Columbine, I am especially praying for you and the other ministers. I know you have been drained through all of this and I am asking the Lord to send you strength, wisdom, and comfort to help you in the weeks and months ahead.

J.H.

Pastor Porter,

I am an 8th grade student in Kentucky. I read the e-mail that had the news report on it. I thought it was very sad to feel what they went through. Our youth leader has been teaching from Matthew 5:37. It says to let your "yes be yes" and your "no be no." I am praying that God would help me do that, just like the girl at Columbine. Even if it requires to give up my life. My prayers will still be with the victims' families, Columbine High School, and the community.

C.P.

Hi Pastor Porter,

I'm 17 years old and from San Antonio, Texas. Somebody forwarded your message to me… I just wanted you to know there's yet another youth out there who wants to help take up the torch… Thanks for remembering that we're out here. It's easy to be blinded by the horror of what happened and forget about the rest. I'm glad somebody still has a positive outlook. Lots of people are still praying and I'm one of 'em. Thank you for your time.

N.T.

Dear Pastor:

I am an attorney in Southern New Jersey and I have just been for-warded a copy of a letter you wrote about Rachel's testimony and funeral. It has reinforced my decision to leave the practice of law to serve our Father through my church in an evangelism and outreach ministry. Thank you, and know that the "torch" has been picked up here in New Jersey; it is time that we are all "about our Father's business."

G.S.

Hi Pastor Bruce,

I received a forward on my e-mail that was an e-mail that you sent out. I must say that what happened in Colorado is being felt all over the nation. I am from Florida and attend school in Alabama. I myself do not know if I would've had the courage of looking death in the face and saying that YES I BELIEVE IN GOD!!! But, this strength that these students showed has changed my life forever. Our prayers are that we and the rest of the Youth of this Nation do rise up and take the torch that those who died left behind.

R.S.

Dear Pastor Bruce,

How my heart breaks and rejoices at the same time when I read of the events during the funeral of Rachel. I know God is speaking to us as a nation. We need to become more committed to what we believe. We need to spread the Gospel now more than ever. I pray that we will not soon forget what happened there. Tennessee is many miles from Littleton, but we are praying for you and your commu-nity. We must all pray that this will turn our Nation around and the Gospel of Christ will be preached everywhere, yes, even in our schools! God Bless you—a friend in Christ in Tennessee.

S.G.

My dear Pastor Porter,

…We watched all of Rachel's funeral with you… We cried when you cried and laughed when you laughed. I watched as you asked the young people in the audience who would pick up the torch that Rachel dropped and carry it and was so pleased as to how many of them stood. You are so right, we must teach our young people and older, as well, to take a stand. Unless we do, this will continue to happen. This just tears out my heart…

S.K. & M.K.

Pastor Porter—

I attend Southwest Baptist University… My heart is hurting for you all. I have been impressed with Rachel's story, as well as her brother Craig. He seems like such a strong young man. Thank you for sharing with us the story of Rachel and challenging us to take up our torch. I will forward it to my friends and encourage them to "take up their torch!" I will be praying for you all in Littleton.

S.B.

Pastor,

I read your account today. I don't know how I got it, but it moved me. I am an associate pastor to children. I too want kids to take up that torch and be a light for all the world to see… Please be aware that I am praying for you and that community. I believe God is taking a tragic episode like this and He is working it out for good. I believe He is bringing about a revival not only in Littleton, but throughout the world because of the lives of these kids.

S.S.

Dear Bruce Porter,

I want to thank you for writing that e-mail about the girls who stuck up for God even though it was fatal for some! I am a 9th grader in northern NY and I'm in love with Jesus Christ! This incident woke me up to say the least! It makes me wonder whether or not I would be able to say, "Yes, I believe in Jesus Christ!" I really hope I would be able to! I believe that we need a revival in the youth of America but it has to start here within myself! I along with many others have mourned this loss especially since we lost some Christians!

With Love in Christ,
A.G.

Dear Pastor Porter,

I live in Gainesville, TX. I am a junior in high school and 17 years old. Many of the students at my school were very affected by the Littleton school shooting, because the population was so close to the population of us. Some of them were saying that it could not happen here, but we all know that it is possible deep in our hearts. I was deeply touched by the story about the boy who even though he had just seen his best friends get shot right beside him he gathered a group of people together so that they could pray for their safety and that of their siblings who had been attending school there too. It said that when they did escape the building the other people he was with found all of their brothers and sisters, but his sister had been victim to this unnecessary violence…but all he had to say about it was that she was with God and He would take care of her. God will take care of them all, and I am glad they are all believers. Although I wish someone had told the two boys of God and His sacrifice, before it was too late for them. The Monday following the shooting my school held a moment of silence in the memory of those deceased. All doors to the counselor's offices were open wide, and everyone opened their arms to anyone who needed a hug.

K.P.

Pastor Bruce:

I believe I can say with confidence that it is not just the young who are taking up this torch. I know that this event was meant by the

127

enemy for evil, but I also know the promise that when the enemy comes in like a flood, that the Spirit will raise up a standard against it. It is those like Cassie, Rachel, and Valeen who proudly bear the same banners that Paul, Peter, and Stephen died to defend. God bless you and your work.

S.H.

Pastor Bruce,

You are touching hearts everywhere. It brings tears to my eyes to read your e-mail but it will be put to good use!!!!! ...I will pass your e-mail to all I am able...it is powerful. Thank you! God for His Grace!! God Bless you!!! and Columbine!

B.R.

Pastor Bruce,

God bless you my brother. We are praying for the youth of our nation. May God raise up a mighty army to carry the torch. Because He lives—

T.

Dear Pastor Bruce,

Let me assure you that I will not tire of your updates. I am sharing all of it with my colleagues at work and my church family, as well as my own family. Littleton has been engraved on my heart. May all of us carry the torch to a lost and dying world!...

In His glory,
S.H.

Dear Pastor Bruce:

I am deeply touched and amazed at the strength and courage that God has given you during these perilous times. I will continue to pray for you, and the situation. I am one of those young ones who is not afraid to take a stand for Christ. Not afraid, no matter what the odds may be. Do not worry, and do not fret. This is a new day and age. For the world, a day of unrest and terror. But for us as the Body of Christ, a day of revival and resurgence. And that's just what I plan to start. I've dedicated my life to bringing about a change in this country. I know that it's not by my might or power, but by the Spirit of God that these things can change. I ask that you pray for me, that God would give me, as well as all others, the strength and knowledge to "carry the torch." May God richly bless you, console your heart, and lead you to that Rock that is higher than I. And that Rock is, Jesus Christ.

God Bless.
P.J.

Pastor Bruce,

Thank you for loving the young people of Littleton. I watched the entire funeral service for Rachel and was extremely moved by the service. I teach Senior High Sunday school and volunteer for youth work and I echoed your challenge and the challenge of our Lord to take up the torch that had fallen from Rachel's hand. As I asked the question, heads nodded all over the room…

W.G.

Dear Pastor Bruce,

We all, like so many who have been touched so deeply by the Columbine tragedy, are so thankful for your updates and labors for the Lord. I am a missionary here in the U.S.A. working among Southeast Asian immigrants in Southern California. The ministry is called Southeast Asian Ministry. I am reaching a lot of Asian kids. On the Friday evening following the shooting and with your first e-mail accounting of the events that occurred there at Columbine I read it to the Youth Bible training class that I teach each Friday eve.

The move of the Holy Spirit was profound. The result was all the students making fuller commitments of their lives to the Lord. All of them have since been baptized in the fullness of the Holy Spirit…and two of them have publicly stated they will gladly take up the torch and stand for Christ even if it means death. These have become the most awesome bold witnesses for the Lord that this ministry has ever seen. Three of the five kids have committed themselves to full-time ministry unto the Lord and are growing so fast in Him it is hard to keep up with them. To God be the glory… Thank you again for your obedience to the Lord in all that you are doing… For His glory,

L.G.

Thank you, Pastor Bruce, for this moving account. Millions of believers share your same passion and intercessory cry for not only justice but revival. I will share this with our congregation and with 350+ young people who gather every Wednesday night for what we call Generation Church. They will pick up the bloodstained torch!

Pastor Wendell Smith
The City Church
Seattle, WA

Resources for The Martyrs' Torch

Torchgrab Youth Ministries
P.O. Box 621372
Littleton, CO 80162
Website: www.torchgrab.org
E-mail: torchgrab@pcisys.net

The Columbine Redemption
Darrell Scott (Rachel Scott's father)
Website: www.thecolumbineredemption.com

Challenge 2000 c/o/ National Network of Youth Ministries
12335 World Trade Drive Suite 16
San Diego, CA 92128 (619) 615-8580
Website: www6.gospelcom.net/every/school
Website: www.nnym.org
Website: challenge2222@nnym.org

Teen Mania
P.O. Box 2000 Garden Valley, TX 75771
1-800-299-TEEN or 1-800-390-FIRE
Website: www.teenmania.org
E-mail: info@teenmania.org

Eastman Curtis Ministries
P.O. Box 470290
Tulsa, OK 74147
(918) 259-9080
Website: www.eastmancurtis.com
E-mail: mail@eastmancurtis.com

Revival Generation
P.O. Box 3288
Englewood, CO 80155-3288
(303) 689-0432
Website: www.revivalgen.org
E-mail: revivalgn@aol.com

High Impact Ministries
P.O. Box 50003
Glendale, Arizona 85312
1-800-72-YOUTH
Website: www.cellgroup.com
E-mail: hiimpact@cellgroup.com

Weiner Ministries Intl.
P.O. Box 1799
Gainesville, FL 32602
(352) 375-4455
Website: www.youthnow.org (Rock America Youth Rallies)
E-mail: Youthnow@aol.com

Forward Edge International
15121-A NE 72nd Avenue
Vancouver, WA 98686
(360) 574-3343
Website: www.forwardedge.org
E-mail: fwdedge@wa-net.com

National Council on Bible Curriculum in Public Schools
Elizabeth Reddener, Founder and President
P.O. Box 9743
Greensboro, NC 27429
Website: www.bibleinschools.org
E-mail: bible1@gte.net
(336) 272-3799

Joy International
P.O. Box 90
Pine, CO 80470
Website: www.joy.org
E-mail: Info@joy.org
(303) 838-7100

Hyoung Chang, *The Denver Post*

Torchgrab Youth Ministries

P.O. Box 621372

Littleton, CO 80162

Website: www.torchgrab.org

E-mail: torchgrab@pcisys.net

Other Destiny Image *titles* you will enjoy reading

THE BATTLE FOR THE SEED
by Dr. Patricia Morgan.
The dilemma facing young people today is a major concern for all parents. This important book shows God's way to change the condition of the young and advance God's purpose for every nation into the next century.
ISBN 1-56043-099-0

HOW TO RAISE CHILDREN OF DESTINY
by Dr. Patricia Morgan.
This groundbreaking book highlights the intricate link between the rise of young prophets, priests, and kings in the Body of Christ as national leaders and deliverers, and the salvation of a generation.
ISBN 1-56043-134-2

NO MORE SOUR GRAPES
by Don Nori.
Who among us wants our children to be free from the struggles we have had to bear? Who among us wants the lives of our children to be full of victory and love for their Lord? Who among us wants the hard-earned lessons from our lives given freely to our children? All these are not only possible, they are also God's will. You can be one of those who share the excitement and joy of seeing your children step into the destiny God has for them. If you answered "yes" to these questions, the pages of this book are full of hope and help for you and others just like you.
ISBN 0-7684-2037-7

SOLDIERS WITH LITTLE FEET
by Dian Layton.
Every time God pours out His Spirit, the adult generation moves on without its children. Dian pleads with the Church to bring the children into the fullness of God with them and offers practical guidelines for doing so.
ISBN 0-914903-86-1

Available at your local Christian bookstore.

Internet: http://www.reapernet.com